Johnson & Higgins at 150 Years

On the 150th anniversary of the founding of Johnson & Higgins, this book is dedicated to the thousands of people — employees, clients, UNISON partners and underwriters, past and present — who have been part of the company's success.

As the focal point of the company's sesquicentennial celebration, Johnson & Higgins employees around the globe are commemorating Worldwide J&H Day on May 11, 1995, by participating in local efforts to benefit children.

Johnson & Higgins
At 150 Years

By Richard Blodgett

GREENWICH PUBLISHING GROUP, INC.

LYME, CONNECTICUT

© 1995 Johnson & Higgins. All rights reserved.

Printed and bound in the United States of America. No part of this publication may be reproduced or transmitted in any form or by any means, electronic or mechanical, including photocopying, recording, or any information storage and retrieval system now known or to be invented, without permission in writing from Johnson & Higgins, 125 Broad Street, New York, NY 10004, except by a reviewer who wishes to quote brief passages in connection with a review written for inclusion in a magazine, newspaper or broadcast.

Photography credits:
Image on the dust jacket and on pp. 3, 10-11, 14, 15 (top), 18-19, 22 (far left), 24 (left), 25-27, 29, 32, 34 (top), 35, 38, 44, 58 and 108-110 courtesy of The Bettmann Archive; pp. 48-49 photograph by Druckner Hilbert Company; p. 69 photograph by Fabian Bachrach; p. 121 (top) courtesy of Computerworld Smithsonian Awards, © Stan Barouh; pp. 136-138 by Ken Korsh.

All other photographs and historical items courtesy of Johnson & Higgins Archives

Photography of Johnson & Higgins artifacts by Timothy J. Connolly

Produced and published by Greenwich Publishing Group, Inc.
Lyme, Connecticut

Design by Clare Cunningham Graphic Design
Essex, Connecticut

Separation & film assembly by Silver Eagle Graphics, Inc.

Library of Congress Catalog Card Number: 94-80243
ISBN: 0-944641-11-3

First Printing: February 1995

Table of Contents

8 *Timeline*

12 *Chapter One*
The Imperative of Change

18 *Chapter Two*
1845-1945: Roots of a Modern Firm

50 *Chapter Three*
W.H. LaBoyteaux: Tough-Minded Boss

56 *Chapter Four*
The Aging Goose with the Golden Eggs

66 *Chapter Five*
Elmer Jefferson and Dorrance Sexton:
Turning Point in the Company's History

74 *Chapter Six*
Going Global

86 *Chapter Seven*
Dick Purnell: "My Thought Was to
Keep the Momentum Going"

90 *Chapter Eight*
Captives

96 *Chapter Nine*
Bob Hatcher: The Kitchen Table Approach

106 *Chapter Ten*
The Ninety-Eight-Year Handshake

116 *Chapter Eleven*
U.S. Retail in the Pressure Cooker

122 *Chapter Twelve*
"If We're the Best, Why Do We
Have to Change?"

126 *Chapter Thirteen*
David Olsen: Why He Defies the Status Quo

134 *Chapter Fourteen*
Johnson & Higgins... A Celebration of People

139 *Acknowledgments*

140 *Index*

Henry W. Johnson

TIMELINE

1845
Jones & Johnson is established in New York as average adjusters and marine insurance brokers; the founders are Walter Restored Jones, Jr., and Henry Ward Johnson, both 24 years old.

1853
Jones and Johnson dissolve their partnership on the last day of the year.

1854
On January 3, A. Foster Higgins, 22, becomes Johnson's new partner; the firm is renamed Johnson & Higgins.

1855
As its revenues grow, J&H commissions the building of a 140-ton wrecking schooner, the *Henry W. Johnson*.

1861-65
American Civil War.

1862
Secretary of the Navy Gideon Wells retains J&H to raise the Union gunboat *Varuna*, sunk by Confederate warships in the Battle of New Orleans.

1871
The great Chicago fire results in nearly $200 million of property loss; the Chicago conflagration and Boston fire the following year trigger the rapid growth of fire insurance.

1879
The Association of Average Adjusters of the United States is founded; Henry Johnson is elected chairman.

1883
J&H opens its first branch office, in San Francisco, to serve the booming West Coast maritime business.

1885
J&H opens its second branch, in Philadelphia.

1892
J&H establishes a correspondent relationship with Henry Willis & Co., a leading British insurance broker; this relationship will continue for 98 years.

1899
J&H incorporates; A. William Krebs is elected president and chief executive officer, serving one year.

1900-02
Tenure of John Barrett as chief executive.

1902-08
Tenure of James B. Dickson as chief executive.

1906
The San Francisco earthquake kills more than 500 and results in property losses exceeding $325 million; J&H sends the head of its fire adjusting staff to the city for six months to settle claims.

1906
Domestic offices now total eight; J&H opens an office in Montreal, its first outside the United States.

1908-09
Tenure of William Brockie as chief executive.

1910-16
Tenure of William R. Coe as chief executive.

1912
The sinking of the *Titanic*; J&H settles hull insurance claims within 30 days.

1914-18
World War I; a J&H director, William N. Davey, is the only broker on the three-member Advisory Board on War Risk Insurance, established by Congress to advise the Secretary of the Treasury.

1916-47
Tenure of William H. LaBoyteaux as chief executive.

1921
J&H opens a branch in Havana, its first outside the U.S. and Canada; in 1960, the Castro regime will expropriate the office, along with the operations of other insurance firms in Cuba.

1923
J&H enters the reinsurance brokerage business through the acquisition of Albert Willcox & Co., predecessor of today's J&H subsidiary, Willcox Incorporated Reinsurance Intermediaries.

1927
J&H establishes an employee benefits business.

1930s
The Great Depression; J&H implements two across-the-board pay cuts, but does not lay off any employees.

TIMELINE

1939-45
World War II; J&H is appointed servicing broker for marine insurance for the U.S. government.

1945
J&H celebrates its 100th anniversary; approximately one-half of J&H's revenue now comes from non-marine lines, as the firm continues its diversification into the property, casualty and employee benefits areas.

1947-52
Tenure of Elmer F. Hunt as chief executive.

1952-62
Tenure of Elmer L. Jefferson as chief executive.

1954
Following its clients abroad, J&H launches an active program of global expansion with the opening of a joint-venture office in Rio de Janeiro.

1956
The *Andrea Doria* sinks off the coast of Nantucket Island; a J&H subsidiary, Shipowners Claims Bureau, settles all claims on behalf of the ship's owner and its mutual protection and indemnity club.

1962-72
Tenure of Dorrance Sexton as chief executive.

1962
Key trip to Europe by J&H senior executives to begin forging a network of European correspondents.

1968
J&H arranges landmark structured settlement agreement to compensate children with birth defects allegedly caused by the drug thalidomide.

1969
J&H forms a subsidiary in Bermuda to manage the insurance business of captive company clients, establishing an early lead in captives management that it has never relinquished.

1972-81
Tenure of Richard I. Purnell as chief executive.

1981
Through ongoing expansion, J&H now has 36 offices in the United States, eight in Canada and 38 in other countries.

1981-90
Tenure of Robert V. Hatcher, Jr., as chief executive.

1982
Formation of UNISON, the global alliance of J&H and its correspondents.

1984
Formation of Johnson & Higgins/Kirke-Van Orsdel in Des Moines to coordinate and administer mass-market insurance products for corporate and association clients.

1989
San Francisco is rocked by a major earthquake; J&H helps settle client claims.

1990-
Tenure of David A. Olsen as chief executive.

1991
J&H establishes a London brokerage subsidiary following the breakup of its correspondent relationship with Willis Faber.

1991
J&H launches a companywide Quality initiative.

1992
In May, riots in South Central Los Angeles cause massive property damage; in August, Hurricane Andrew devastates southern Florida; these and other events precipitate a record year of insured losses; J&H is active in settling claims and helping clients find coverage as underwriting capacity is stretched to the limits.

1993
J&H names its first managing principals, broadening ownership of the firm beyond the members of the board of directors.

1994
J&H worldwide revenues reach $1 billion.

1994
A severe earthquake strikes Los Angeles; J&H mobilizes to settle clients' claims.

1995
J&H celebrates its 150th anniversary.

J&H today: 8,400 employees; 120 J&H offices and 135 offices of UNISON partners in 62 countries; active participation in an array of insurance brokerage and consulting services; a culture of teamwork and client service.

This photograph of the New York waterfront was taken in the early 1860s, when Johnson & Higgins was well on its way to establishing itself as the dominant marine insurance broker and average adjuster in the United States. Today, building on its marine heritage of innovation, integrity and client service, J&H is a premier global insurance broker serving corporate clients with a full array of services.

JOHNSON & HIGGINS AT 150 YEARS

1.

The Imperative of Change

There is a boiling, evolving change taking place at Johnson & Higgins. I think it will require many years to unfold. And I wouldn't predict for one moment how it will play out." Those words are spoken by a veteran J&H employee, Charles M. Binford, who retired in 1993. Change is being driven, he asserts, by new and evolving client needs and by an intense pressure on profit margins throughout the insurance brokerage industry.

James W. McElvany, who heads the firm's Los Angeles office, expresses a similar view. "You can't be theoretical about change," he insists. "You have to step up to the plate and commit the people and resources to what you think your future is."

Two areas of focus in many J&H offices, including Los Angeles, are the development of new alternative risk-financing techniques and major investments in interactive software systems that link the underwriter, the client and J&H. "These are two of the decisions we have made to keep us on the front edge in Los Angeles," McElvany states. "If we are wrong, we will be spinning our wheels. If we are right, and I think we are, we will remain the dominant broker in Southern California for years and years and years."

There was a time when change came slowly to the

insurance brokerage industry, and for good reason. As in many other service businesses, the most successful insurance brokers were exceptionally profitable — and J&H, the nation's oldest broker, was the most profitable of them all. In the mid-1940s, when the Internal Revenue Service disclosed the salaries of the highest-paid executives in the United States, three of the top ten were officers of Johnson & Higgins. "The business was so profitable you couldn't really mess it up," one J&H director comments. Profit margins in some years exceeded 50 percent. Given those circumstances, who would want to change?

But the days of milk and honey ended years ago, when increased competition began to sweep through the industry. As a result, J&H has been traveling a nonstop course of change since the late 1950s, transforming itself from a successful old-line firm in a shrinking business — marine insurance brokerage — to a modern, growing, multiline brokerage and consulting company with global operations.

Clients are now raising their expectations another notch. "Clients want more and more from us," David A. Olsen, chairman and chief executive officer, states. In fact, J&H reached a milestone in 1994 when its worldwide revenues exceeded $1 billion for the first time. "Unfortunately," he adds, "some clients want to pay less and less for the service they get. This is not unique to our business. It is the same pressure everybody faces today — in manufacturing as well as throughout the service industry." He adds, "Two years ago I told our people we had to be the best in everything we do. I also said that, in being the best, we might not always charge the lowest prices. Now I realize I was wrong. We not only have to be the best, but our prices have to be as competitive as anybody's." Olsen sees a shakeout taking place in the insurance brokerage industry and says J&H must position itself not only to survive but to capitalize on the opportunities this shakeout is creating.

Don Carlson, manager of the St. Louis office, remarks, "Product, price, delivery, quality and service — that's what our clients want. We have to work harder and smarter, but it's good for our industry because it makes everybody do a better job."

At the same time, Olsen observes, "Change is a delicate balance. We must be careful not to change what shouldn't be changed. The name Johnson & Higgins stands for certain values, including professionalism and absolute integrity. Our relationships with clients and underwriters are based on these values." More than three decades ago, a J&H director, David H. Winton, captured the essence of the company in a memo that is as valid today as it was back then. Describing the firm's dealings with underwriters, Winton said that each J&H'er must be "shrewd but not cunning, capable of high level intelligence and debate without controversy, confident without being overbearing, knowledgeable without being a 'know-it-all,' a listener as well as a speaker and, above all, courteous in speech and attitude, honest and straightforward in every market relationship." These words have withstood the test of time as an appropriate way to run any business.

Serving Corporate Clients

J&H serves clients in a particular market segment: large and mid-sized organizations, primarily corporations. Over the years, J&H has brokered coverages for such diverse insureds as the oceanliner *Titanic*, the business properties of Andrew Mellon, the racehorse *Secretariat* and each new generation of Boeing jetliners. In 1959, when Time, Incorporated, acquired the rights to the stories of the seven original Mercury astronauts — and agreed to insure each of their lives for $1 million — J&H placed the coverage, certainly one of the more difficult-to-analyze risks imaginable. "It gave us a linkage to the astronauts, in those early days of the space program, which was something special," says Rodney D. Day III, a J&H director. With its UNISON partners, J&H has brokered all manner of complex global coverages, including those for the Olympic Games in France, Spain and Norway and now for the 1996 Summer Olympics to be held in Atlanta and the 1998 Winter Olympics to be held in Japan.

J&H brokered hull insurance for the ill-fated *Titanic*. This drawing of the *Titanic* calamity is titled "Women and Children First."

When Time, Incorporated, acquired rights to the life stories of the seven original Mercury astronauts, it agreed to insure each of their lives for $1 million, turning to J&H to place this coverage.

Andrew Mellon was a long-time J&H client, arranging insurance for his business properties through the firm.

"Bloodline" insurance is a specialty of J&H's Richmond, Virginia, office. Triple-crown winner *Secretariat* was one of the many famous thoroughbreds for which J&H has placed coverage.

J&H is known for its ability to arrange large and complex coverages, including property and casualty insurance for each new generation of Boeing jetliners.

There are larger brokerage firms. J&H ranks number five in the world in terms of revenues (it would rank number two if the revenues of its UNISON partners were included). But size alone is not an indication of the firm's reputation and clout. J&H is one of the premier firms in the corporate market, serving half the *Fortune* 500 companies. "It's the ability to serve that top end of the spectrum that sets us apart," according to Olsen.

The problem — and the opportunity — is this: The evolving dynamics of this market segment are similar to the watershed that occurred in commercial banking some 15 years ago. "For the banks, profit margins in their traditional business — lending to multinational companies — were eroding," notes Joseph D. Roxe, chief financial officer of J&H. "And the smart banks said, 'I have a choice. I can change the quality of the loans I make and thereby increase the yield. Or I can diversify into other related businesses.'" Some banks prospered by emphasizing corporate services. A number of others did not adjust and had to merge to survive. "I think the insurance brokerage industry is heading along a parallel course," Roxe explains. "Profit margins in our traditional business, property and casualty insurance brokerage, are eroding. So we have to run the company smarter. We have to reduce our costs. And we have to identify other insurance services that will produce better rates of return."

One recent venture involved a strategic alliance with Goldman, Sachs & Co. to raise $450 million of capital for a newly formed property catastrophe reinsurance company in Bermuda, responding to the current demand for increased worldwide catastrophic insurance capacity. "The trend is to look for ways to use our capital and expertise in nontraditional areas that address the needs of clients," Roxe states.

To foster change, J&H has launched a companywide Quality initiative — one of the most interesting and innovative quality programs in a service-company setting (see Chapter 12). The purpose is to challenge traditional ways of doing business within J&H and to tap the ideas and talents of the company's 8,400 employees worldwide. Christine LaSala, who heads the J&H New York office, notes that when J&H first opened its doors 150 years ago it was an average adjusting firm (apportioning liability for maritime losses). The firm then moved into transaction-based insurance brokerage. "Now we are becoming more of a broker-consultant," she says. "Our work is becoming less transaction-oriented and more risk-management-consulting based. And indeed, our Quality initiative has verified that clients want more of a consulting approach and less emphasis on transactions alone."

To hear about all these challenges, one might think that J&H is a company in turmoil. To the contrary, J&H remains consistently profitable. It is debt-free. Retained earnings currently exceed $300 million. Revenue growth remains strong. And investment continues to be financed entirely from cash flow.

Explaining the need for change, Olsen recalls the saying, "Whom the gods want to destroy they give 40 years of success." He makes clear, "We are not anywhere near going broke or folding up or having to merge. But the time to look hard at the future is when things are going well."

PRIVATE OWNERSHIP

One of the special attributes of J&H is its private ownership. Among the world's largest insurance brokerage firms, it is the only one to remain privately owned. This has created something of a mystique about the firm, since its management deliberations and financial results are not disclosed publicly.

Although often thought of as a partnership, J&H is in fact a corporation owned by a current total of 30 directors and 19 managing principals. These individuals, whose positions are similar to those of the partners in a law firm, are the senior officers of the company. In an unusual arrangement that dates back to the firm's incorporation in 1899, directors buy into the firm inexpensively. "The stock arrangements are established so anybody who is selected can afford to buy shares," says Gardner M. Mundy, general counsel. "It is a unique and democratic process. You don't have to be wealthy to be elected to the J&H board. You do have to show you can make a significant contribution to the business."

Directors can serve until age 60, or until 62 if they have been on the board less than 15 years. They must then retire and sell their shares back to the firm, receiving payments over the ensuing ten years based on J&H financial results. This arrangement provides an incentive for directors to choose worthy successors who will manage the business effectively. In addition, it offers an efficient means to keep J&H's stock out of estates and entirely in the hands of people who are active in the business. Typically each December, one or more directors retire and are replaced by senior executives who are elected to the board. Over the past 96 years, since the firm switched to a corporate structure, 144 individuals have served on the J&H board in a continuous process of gradually passing the reins of leadership to new generations of owner/managers.

The chance to reach for the brass ring of board membership is a powerful incentive for many J&H employees, though not the be-all and end-all it once was. In fact, some senior employees now earn more than junior directors. And Binford contends, in any case, that the power of the firm vests broadly across the ranks of senior employees, not just with the board. "In my opinion, if you were to identify 150 people driving change," he says, "you would get a number of directors, but also a lot of managing principals, senior vice presidents and others. The power of Johnson & Higgins does not reside entirely with the board. It vests significantly in that select group of people who have total access to the board members but do not belong to the board themselves, and have the entrepreneurial freedom to develop new business ideas and creative solutions."

Many at J&H swear by the firm's tightly knit structure of private ownership, and there is a widespread belief that this structure is a catalyst for the company's strong culture of employee teamwork and client service. "There are no superstars who pursue their own agendas," according to Mike J. Hudson, the Property Department manager in the Los Angeles office. "We operate as a team and everybody wants to uphold their end of the deal. Everybody worries about satisfying the client. We can do that because, as a private company, we can concentrate on fewer audiences. We don't have public shareholders to worry about."

Private ownership is not necessarily forever. Over the past five decades, there have been occasional suggestions by directors that the firm go public. Although these suggestions have always been rejected by a majority of the board, going public would increase the firm's access to capital. "There is no evidence at this point that we are capital constrained," Roxe reports. "In the future, if we were to expand into new businesses, we might need additional capital, whether it's through the public sale of stock or a private placement with insurance companies or something of that nature. But until we get to that point, there is no need to change from being private."

Olsen adds, "We would feel sad if we were driven to it [going public], unless it involved an incredibly wonderful opportunity for our people and our clients and the future of the firm."

THE J&H VISION

Few organizations in the United States have a tradition as long or proud as that of Johnson & Higgins. It has grown and evolved through decades of change and has consistently been a leader in its industry. It is one of the largest privately owned enterprises in the U.S. and one of the world's preeminent insurance brokers.

Many businesses today have a "corporate vision." What is the vision of J&H? "It is very simple," Olsen responds. "Our vision is to remain big and growing, to improve our profitability, to remain global, to remain the best in the business. Period. That's it. Of course, that connotes serving clients well, getting new business, being efficient and so on."

Let's take a closer look at this 150-year-old firm. Let's delve beneath the surface. Let's "demystify" J&H and see how it got to be the firm it is today.

2.
1845-1945: Roots of a Modern Firm

I*magine yourself, if you will, living a century and a half ago in New York, a city bursting at the seams with energy. The human drama, in all its glory and pathos, would unfold before your very eyes. A British observer, standing at the corner of Broadway and Wall Street, was astonished to find "driving, jostling and elbowing... and the crashing noises of [horse-drawn] omnibuses flying in all directions." Streets were paved with cobblestone, or not yet paved at all. Gas lamps were being installed to light the night. Wealth and poverty existed side by side: the magnificent Astor House hotel, overlooking City Hall, was one of the first buildings in the world to feature plumbing on every floor. Not half a mile to the north lay the seedy Five Points district, a hotbed of scoundrels and thieves.*

By the mid-nineteenth century, New York was America's most populous city and leading seaport. The late nineteenth century view, right, shows West Street along the Hudson River docks.

J&H co-founder Walter Restored Jones, Jr., far left, came from a prominent family of Long Island merchants and jurists. Near left, family members gathered at the Greenwich, Connecticut, home of Andrew Foster Higgins and wife Sara to celebrate the couple's 50th wedding anniversary on May 5, 1902.

New York was, above all, a center of commerce. Since the opening of the Erie Canal in 1825, New York had become the gateway for trade with the Middle West, creating an economic boom and giving rise to a prosperous merchant class. Majestic sailing ships docked at the city's wharfs to unload and pick up cargo; their masts, flying colorful flags from around the world, ringed lower Manhattan like a forest. Drawn by opportunity, immigrants were flooding to the city in unprecedented numbers. As a result, New York's population surged from 391,000 in 1840 to 696,000 just ten years later. On the Lower East Side, the first tenements were being built to house the endless waves of eager arrivals.

Onto this dynamic stage stepped two young men, Walter Restored Jones, Jr., and Henry Ward Johnson, who were swept up in the entrepreneurial fervor of the time. Both had entered the insurance business as teenagers and had worked together as clerks at the Atlantic Mutual Insurance Company in lower Manhattan. In 1845, when both were 24 years old, they quit their jobs to form a partnership in a small office at 90 Wall Street. Early portraits show them with thick black beards and stern visages, perhaps to conceal their youthful looks.

Jones came from a family of merchants and jurists who had settled on Long Island in 1695. Of Welsh ancestry, he had many relatives in the insurance business, including his uncle, Walter Restored Jones, a lifelong bachelor who served for many years as president of Atlantic Mutual. The middle name Restored, shared by uncle and nephew, was coined by the uncle's mother (Walter Jr.'s grandmother) who had lost an earlier son named Walter. When her next child was a son, she is said to have proclaimed, "Walter has been restored to us!" The phrase stuck, and the newborn was christened Walter Restored.

Johnson was born in Hartford, Connecticut, and had journeyed to New York as a youth in search of work. Of the two partners, Johnson would prove to be the more energetic and assertive, leading the firm through its first three decades.

Johnson & Higgins was founded in this building at 90 Wall Street in lower Manhattan. The structure was demolished in 1901.

1845: The Year J&H Was Founded

- James Polk was inaugurated as the 11th President of the United States.
- Florida and Texas were admitted to the Union.
- The national debt totaled $16 million.
- The first Yankee clipper, the *Rainbow*, was launched in New York.
- The United States Naval Academy was founded at Annapolis, Maryland.
- Edgar Allen Poe achieved fame with "The Raven."
- Baseball rules were codified by Alexander Cartwright.
- The first telegraph cable was laid across the English Channel, following invention of the telegraph by Samuel Morse a year earlier.
- The first U.S. postage stamp was issued by New York City postmaster Robert Morris.

Average Adjusters & Insurance Brokers

The two men hung out their shingle as Jones & Johnson, Average Adjusters & Insurance Brokers. (As we shall see, Jones & Johnson would soon become Johnson & Higgins.) Although insurance brokerage was part of the firm's business from the start, its relative importance was initially very small. Jones and Johnson were both trained as adjusters, and the firm's activities were concentrated in that field. In any event, there was not much demand for insurance brokerage in the 1840s. The widespread acceptance of this function lay in the future.

Marine insurance was the dominant form of indemnity in the 1840s. To meet the needs of an expanding American-flag fleet, some 75 insurance companies had been organized in seaports along the eastern seaboard. Shipowners in ports like New York and Charleston found it convenient to deal directly with these local companies, which had offices near the docks. Before a ship set sail, the owner would purchase insurance for the craft and merchants would do so for their goods on board. Terms of coverage were brief and to the point. Insurance contracts were often so succinct they could be written on a single sheet of paper. Given the fact that contracts were short and simple, who needed a broker? Demand for brokers to represent the interests of the insured would emerge later, as the scope and complexity of contracts increased.

Average Adjusting: What It Is, How It Started

While insurance brokerage was still in its infancy in the 1840s, average adjusting was a well-established profession. In a seaport like New York, where the main economic activity was shipping and shipbuilding, there were dozens of adjusters earning a good living. "Average" has a particular definition in this context. Derived from the French *avarie*, meaning damage to a ship or cargo, it is the marine underwriter's word for loss.

Average adjusting is a comparatively modern outgrowth of a principle that originated more than 3,000 years ago in the earliest days of commerce on the Mediterranean. The Mediterranean was stormy, ships were often overloaded and the hazards of the sea, consequently, were great. When a vessel appeared to be in danger of sinking, every sailor knew just what to do: lighten the load by dumping cargo into the sea or cutting down the mast and rigging. Quick, decisive action was imperative. There was no time for hesitation or debate. The most accessible cargo, usually that on deck, would be jettisoned first. Some merchants might suffer large or even total losses, but the lives of the passengers and the cargo of other merchants would be saved. It seemed only fair, however, that all interested parties should share in these losses. In fact, this doctrine was formalized in the maritime codes of Rhodes nine centuries before the birth of Christ and has been recognized in maritime commerce ever since. A marine loss involving the sacrifice of vessel or cargo for the common good, where the costs are distributed among all parties, is called general average. In the United States, this term first appeared in 1773 in a Connecticut case in which the jettison of horses from on deck was allowed to be included in the losses apportioned to all.

The concept was and is simple. On the other hand, the application of the concept grew increasingly complex as ships became larger and began to carry cargoes for hundreds or even thousands of merchants. This eventually made necessary the use of disinterested persons, informed in all the customs, usages and intricacies of general average, to gather the facts, weigh the merits of each case and decide the amount of damages and their proper allocation. Such a person is called an average adjuster and is selected by the shipowner, who is charged with protecting the interests of all concerned. General average is not insurance, but a loss shared by all parties, whether insured or not. Of course, there are many marine disasters in which no voluntary sacrifice is made, cases in which all damage results from an accident. Reimbursement then becomes a matter of separate loss adjustments between the individual parties and their insurance companies.

As it grew, the young company became the predomi-

From Candles to Electricity in

Because we live today in an era of explosive technological change, it is easy to overlook the fact that technology advanced rapidly, too, in the mid-nineteenth century, as indicated by the telephone, typewriter, transatlantic telegraph and other innovations. Johnson & Higgins was quick to embrace them all.

Another significant change involved office lighting, an area in which J&H co-founder Foster Higgins had some personal experience. In 1850, while still employed by Atlantic Mutual Insurance Company, he helped draft the so-called "candle petition." At the time, many offices were lit by sperm-whale-oil candles, but gas was gaining popularity. The 14 clerks at Atlantic Mutual asked "respectfully" that gas lights be installed at their desks, couching the issue in economic terms. "Aside from the injury to our eyes from the constant flickering of the light from candles," their petition to management stated, "it is believed that after the first cost of the pipes, a great saving could be effected in the cost of lights by the use of gas in lieu of candles...."

Atlantic Mutual agreed, and gas lights were in place shortly thereafter — with the injunction that they be turned off after hours to avoid wasting money. Johnson &

Far left, this nineteenth century woodcut is titled "Lamplighter." Shown above is an early J&H office with roll-top desks.

Three Decades

Thomas Edison built the world's first electric power plant near Wall Street in 1882. Businesses immediately recognized the benefits of electric power, including better and more dependable lighting.

Higgins was equally cost-conscious about gas lighting. Employee regulations issued by J&H in 1862 contain the warning, "Each person, upon leaving his desk at the close of business for the day, must see that the gas at his desk is turned off, and will be held responsible therefor."

Gas technology was, in turn, soon supplanted. In 1882, Thomas Edison built the world's first electric power plant on Pearl Street near the offices of Johnson & Higgins. Nearly every company in lower Manhattan, including J&H, soon switched to the efficient new energy source, which has remained the standard ever since.

nant adjusting firm in the United States, handling not only complex general average cases but also resolving insurance claims resulting from hull and cargo losses. By the mid-1850s, over a single 12-month period, the firm adjusted 66 cases involving Atlantic Mutual and an unknown number involving other parties. Statistics do not exist for subsequent years, but almost certainly the number of cases handled by J&H increased dramatically during the second half of the nineteenth century. Indeed, Henry Johnson became one of the giants of the profession. Upon the formation of the Association of Average Adjusters of the United States in 1879, he was elected its first chairman. Six of the association's first 22 chairmen were, in fact, from J&H. Andrew Foster Higgins, a J&H partner from 1854 to 1887, was another of the towering figures. It was said that he adjusted 10,000 cases over the course of his career, equivalent to one case per working day year in and year out! Higgins could not possibly have resolved all 10,000 cases by himself. Most likely, he reviewed and approved the findings and supervised employees who took care of the details. Nonetheless, of the 10,000 cases, the findings of fewer than 20 were appealed to the courts, reflecting well on his knowledge and abilities, which were legendary. One of his colleagues said that Higgins, "realizing that at some time or other every possible question relating to marine insurance had been passed upon," assembled the most complete collection of marine decisions ever gathered and then fired all of J&H's lawyers because they weren't needed any more! Whether that statement was literally true is impossible to know today.

But no matter. However you slice the cake, Johnson & Higgins was unequalled in the average adjusting business. There was no other firm quite like it. Average adjusting remained an important enterprise for J&H into the mid-twentieth century. Even today, the firm offers these services through its Shipowners Claims Bureau subsidiary, although the volume of business is greatly reduced from the profession's glory days of the past. David Olsen notes that J&H began with two average adjusters, Jones and Johnson. At the peak of this activity, the firm had as many as 100. Today, it is back to two.

The commercial life of New York was centered on the South Street docks, which were visited by colorful vessels from around the world. Reflecting its maritime origins, Johnson & Higgins' New York headquarters has always been located near the lower Manhattan waterfront.

J&H's origins in average adjusting continue to influence its culture. Average adjusting requires in-depth knowledge, unquestioned integrity and singleness of purpose in meeting the needs of clients. That combination has remained a winning formula for J&H.

AGE OF THE YANKEE CLIPPERS

The two partners, Jones and Johnson, could not have chosen a better time to start their business: the great era of the Yankee clippers was just dawning. Much has been written about these splendid vessels, which ruled the seas for nearly two decades. Prior to the launching of the first Yankee clipper in 1845, even the fastest sailing vessel took nearly 200 days to complete the voyage from New York to San Francisco around Cape Horn. The sleek, graceful clippers cut that time in half. The most famous clipper of them all, *The Flying Cloud*, sliced crisply through the waves to make the voyage in 89 days, a sailing-vessel record that was not broken until 1989 by a yacht incorporating the most advanced twentieth century sail technology.

Above, stevedores unload a ship at a New York dock in an 1887 woodcut. Right, an unidentified clipper ship. Yankee clippers ruled the seas from the mid-1840s to the early 1860s, bringing prosperity to the U.S. maritime industry — and to Johnson & Higgins.

These were wonderful times for the American maritime industry. Propelled by the fast new ships as well as by the discovery of gold in California, American-fleet tonnage quadrupled between 1845 and 1861. We must remember also, however, that the sea can be a cruel master. As might be expected, the clippers did not always enjoy safe passage. In one year alone, the *San Francisco*, ravaged by Pacific storms, drifted to the entrance of the port for which she was named and sank; the *Trade Wind* was lost in a collision at sea; and the *Oriental* foundered in Chinese waters. As tragic as these and other losses were, they fueled demand for adjusting services. Responding to the great surge of the American maritime industry in the late 1840s and early 1850s, Jones and Johnson quickly built a good-sized, profitable business.

Then in 1853 something unexpected happened: the two men went their separate ways. Maybe they parted company as friends. Or perhaps the partnership was torn apart by a dispute. We don't know the answer. Even

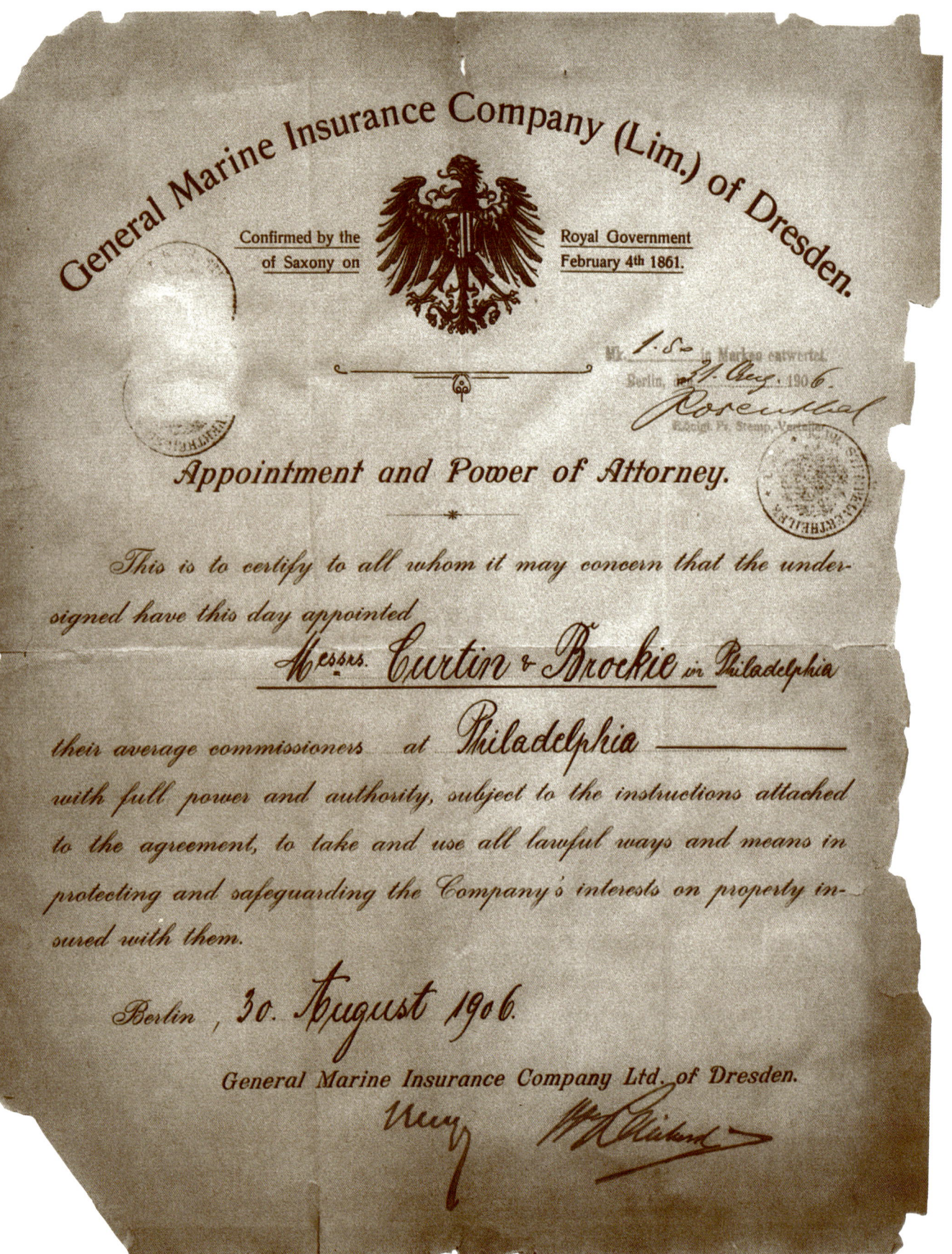

With this power of attorney, Transatlantic Marine Insurance Company of Berlin, Germany, appointed J&H as its agent to settle claims in Philadelphia. The power of attorney was issued to Curtin & Brockie, the name under which J&H operated in Philadelphia for many years. No other U.S. firm was more widely employed by marine insurers to settle claims than J&H.

The Yankee clippers were said to carry "a veritable cloud of sails." It was only natural, therefore, that the greatest clipper of them all, pictured here, would be named the *Flying Cloud*. Owned by a New York firm, the *Flying Cloud* was a frequent and spectacular visitor to the city's South Street piers. There is no record to indicate whether J&H placed insurance for the speedy vessel herself, although it certainly must have done so for some of her cargo.

A. Foster Higgins was a long-time leader of the company who was known nationally for his involvement in Republican politics. An individual of great charm and intelligence, he was only 22 years old when he became a J&H partner in 1854, serving more than three decades until his retirement in 1887. Pictured above is his wife Sara.

assuming the reasons were revealed at the time, they are now lost to history.

Jones went into business for himself, retiring several years later at a relatively young age. He died in 1884 in his 63rd year. Johnson forged ahead with the partnership, inviting a talented young employee, A. Foster Higgins, to take Jones' place. The new partnership, formed on January 3, 1854, was called Johnson & Higgins.

Andrew Foster Higgins

Just as youth had not been a handicap for Jones and Johnson when they established their firm, neither was it for Higgins. He was just 22 years old when he assumed the mantle of partnership. By all accounts, he was exceptionally bright and ambitious and had a natural head for business. Descended from a family of well-to-do early American settlers (his great-grandfather had been a general in the Revolutionary War), Higgins was born and raised in Macon, Georgia, where his father was a cotton merchant. After completing private school in his native state, young Higgins ventured north to attend Colgate University and then Columbia University, but was forced to leave college when his father suffered financial reversals. He was only 15. Remaining in New York, he took the first job offered — as a clerk in a tailor's shop — and six months later, in 1847, joined Jones & Johnson, where he learned the rudiments of average adjusting. In 1848 he left for Atlantic Mutual, just down the street at 47 Wall, spending the next three years at the company led by Walter Jones' uncle before returning to Jones & Johnson in 1851.

Three years after that, in accepting Johnson's invitation of partnership, he became a principal in a business that was already highly successful. Indeed, not long afterward, J&H commissioned the building of a 140-ton schooner to salvage ships and cargo at sea — an investment well beyond the means of almost any other adjusting firm of the time. The vessel, named the *Henry W. Johnson*, measured 97 feet from stem to stern and was built at a shipyard on New York's East River.

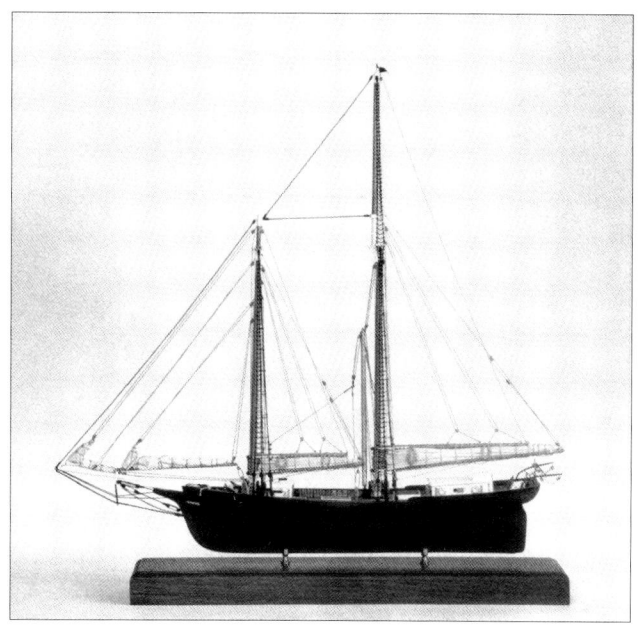

The *Henry W. Johnson* was a 97-foot wrecking schooner commissioned by Johnson & Higgins in the 1850s to salvage ships and cargo at sea. Because no original plans or pictures of the ship are known to exist today, James M. Vaccarino, a senior vice president in the Boston office, built this model based on pictures of similar ships. Vaccarino constructed the model in the early 1980s at the request of J&H chairman Robert Hatcher. Today, the model is displayed in the executive offices of J&H in New York.

The Civil War brought America's maritime industry to a virtual halt, ushering in a difficult period for Johnson & Higgins. Pictured is the interior of Fort Sumter shortly after it was captured by Confederate forces.

The firing on Fort Sumter on April 12, 1861, and the Civil War that followed brought the boom days of the American merchant fleet to an abrupt end. Fortunately, J&H had already achieved enough size and staying power to survive the lean years of the war. The two partners, Johnson and Higgins — one a New Englander, the other from the deep south — managed to put aside any political differences and keep the business going.

Like most businesses of the time, J&H ran a tight ship and expected a full day's work from its employees. Company regulations from the Civil War era state that clerks (as all employees were then called) had to arrive by 8:30 a.m. in the summer and 9 a.m. in the winter and could not leave before 6 p.m., and even then only if their work was done. The regulations warned that "no loud talking, laughing or gossiping will be permitted." Moreover, smoking was "strictly prohibited," as it is again today in New York and many other J&H offices.

On May 13, 1862, in one of the more unusual events in the firm's history, J&H was engaged by Secretary of the Navy Gideon Wells to send an agent to New Orleans to examine the stranded Union warship *Varuna* with a view toward restoring her to combat condition. The *Varuna* had taken damage from a Confederate gunboat during the Battle of New Orleans. According to J&H's 100th anniversary book, published in 1945, "Pursuant to Secretary Wells' order, the *Varuna* was raised by Johnson & Higgins, repaired and put into service."

AFTER THE CIVIL WAR

Upon the war's end, J&H resumed its growth. By now, insurance brokerage was winning its first tentative acceptance. In his classic 1919 book, *Marine Insurance*, William D. Winter, president of Atlantic Mutual Insurance Company from 1934 to 1946, said the progress of the brokerage industry was slow at first. "Merchant and shipowner had to be persuaded that the broker could serve them as well or better than they

One of Johnson & Higgins' most visible actions during the Civil War was the raising of the U.S.S. *Varuna* on orders from Navy Secretary Gideon Wells. The *Varuna*, shown here, disabled four Confederate gunboats in the Battle of New Orleans before taking damage and sinking. Presumably the company sent its wrecking schooner, the *Henry W. Johnson*, to handle the job.

could be served in dealing directly with the underwriter," he wrote. "In time the idea received general acceptance as the problems of overseas commerce became more and more complicated." According to Winter, by the beginning of the twentieth century, most marine coverage in the United States was being negotiated through brokers.

As one of America's first and best-known marine brokers, J&H was unusually well positioned to win the business of merchants and shipowners as they looked to brokers for assistance. The firm gained a special reputation for its ability to place large and unusual risks, the most dramatic example being the hull coverage on the ill-starred *Titanic* in 1912. (Eerily, not only did J&H help place the coverage, but J&H's chief executive at the time, William R. "W.R." Coe, was booked on the return voyage of the liner to England, a passage that would never be made.) Even today, J&H is known for its skill in broking large and unusual coverages, no longer just in the marine field.

The years following the Civil War also saw the marine underwriting market shift to England, as American insurers, still reeling from the dearth of business during the war, fell on hard times. The first British marine insurance company entered New York State about 1871 and was quickly followed by many others. Much of the cargo business to and from the United States continued to be insured in the U.S. market, but hull underwriting gravitated to the U.K., where rates were lower. This added to the complexity of obtaining coverage and was one of the

Legacy of the *Titanic*

As the leading marine insurance broker, Johnson & Higgins has been involved in the aftermath of virtually all the great marine disasters. None was more shocking than the sinking of the *Titanic* on her maiden voyage in April 1912.

The *Titanic* was insured for $5.6 million, of which $4.9 million was hull coverage and $700,000 was disbursement insurance, the latter payable only in the event of a total loss. Coverage had been placed jointly by Willis Faber in Europe and J&H in the U.S. The prospect of the *Titanic* going down had seemed so far-fetched that the disbursement policy had been written at a rate of only 3/8th of one percent, or a premium of $2,630 for the $700,000 of coverage.

Between them, Willis Faber and J&H arranged for all claims to be paid within 30 days of the luxury liner's demise. Though the owners of the ship were reimbursed, the survivors and the heirs of passengers who died did not collect a penny. Under the laws of the time, shipowners could be held liable only with great difficulty for injuries or deaths during a voyage.

What's more, a shipowner's total liability was limited to the value of the vessel after the accident — and all that was left of the *Titanic* were her lifeboats, worth a mere $1,000.

It was not until 22 years later, when the *Morro Castle* burned off the New Jersey coast killing 134 people, that the U.S. government set minimum liability standards for shipowners. U.S. laws now limit a shipowner's total liability to $420 per gross registered ton. The *Titanic* weighed in at 46,300 gross tons, so the maximum liability under this standard would have been some $20 million. However, courts often disregard these limits in cases of negligence, and today's liners sometimes carry $1 billion or more of liability coverage.

Safety measures in the era of the *Titanic* were overrated. Thereafter, ships were equipped with lifeboats for all aboard, more rigid inspections were inaugurated and materials were improved. The palatial trappings of the *Titanic* included highly flammable teak decks and woodburning fireplaces in many of the staterooms. Today, the piano and the cook's chopping block are very often the only wood on a ship.

The *Titanic* was the greatest luxury liner of her time. Her state-of-the-art construction included a double bottom and 16 separate watertight compartments. She could float with any two compartments flooded, and since no one could imagine anything worse than a collision at the juncture of two compartments, she was labeled "unsinkable."

factors prompting insureds to turn to brokers. Faced with the drying-up of the U.S. hull market, J&H engaged a series of British correspondents to place coverage in London, culminating in the formation of its exclusive correspondent relationship with Henry Willis & Co., later Willis, Faber & Co. (see Chapter 10).

Changing of the Guard

On reaching its 50th anniversary in 1895, J&H was clearly the preeminent marine broker in the United States, a position it would hold for many years. The founders were by now gone and the firm was being led by a second generation of partners, most of whom had worked their way up the ranks as average adjusters. The first new partner was A. William Krebs, hired in the 1860s and tapped for partnership in 1874. When founder Henry Johnson died in 1881, John D. Barrett became a partner, joining Higgins and Krebs. Six others were admitted to partnership in the years before the century's end.

Meanwhile, Higgins left in 1887, at age 56, to continue his career as an independent businessman and financier, retaining an ownership interest in J&H even though he was no longer involved in its day-to-day affairs. He became one of the most famous financiers of his time. Active in Republican politics, he gained front-page headlines in 1892 when he announced his intention to vote for the Democratic presidential candidate, Grover Cleveland, in a dispute over the highly protectionist McKinley Tariff Act of 1890. The *New York Times* even made the news of his defection to the Democrats its lead story of the day. Under the headline "Mr. Higgins Also Leaves: He Can Stand the Republican Policy No Longer," the *Times* quoted him as saying that, although he was a life-long protectionist, he objected to the Republican Party's programs to impose tariffs "which are plainly [intended] to pour money into the pockets of capitalists of industries well established."

As an investor and financier, Higgins was well known for his ability to save troubled companies from bankruptcy, being enlisted by none other than J.P. Morgan, Sr., to resuscitate the Knickerbocker Trust Company in one of the great corporate rescue operations of the early twentieth century. Higgins sat on the board of the Knickerbocker, a major New York City bank that faltered in 1907 when it lost money on speculative investments, triggering one of the most severe financial panics in American history. Higgins spearheaded the successful effort to save the Knickerbocker and return it to profitability. By now in his late seventies, this would be his last hurrah before he retired for good. An avid outdoorsman as well as a prosperous businessman, Higgins lived to the ripe old age of 86, dying in 1916 at his Victorian mansion in Greenwich, Connecticut. In a lengthy obituary, the *New York Times* described him as "an adjuster of remarkable ability... a prominent financier... and many times a millionaire."

Why Did J&H Incorporate?

In 1899, the second-generation partners did something for which there is no obvious explanation, even though their action has served J&H extremely well ever since: they incorporated the firm. "The motivation is genuinely unknown to us today," asserts Gardner Mundy, J&H's general counsel. "I can trace the evolution of our corporate charter and all the ownership arrangements with exquisite detail. But why our forebears incorporated the firm, I don't know."

Frederic Howard, who heads J&H's tax staff, notes that the decision to incorporate could not have been motivated by tax considerations, since there was no income tax at the time. Nor was it likely to have been prompted by a desire to shield the partners from liability, since such concerns were not then widespread. "For all we know, they chose to incorporate simply because other companies were doing it," Howard surmises.

In the years following the Civil War, corporations had become the main entities for conducting business in the United States. By 1900, two-thirds of all manufactured goods in the U.S. were produced by corpora-

Johnson & Higgins was incorporated in 1899, more than five decades after its founding. The terms of the company's certificate of incorporation have served J&H well, providing an effective means to keep the company's stock in the hands of owner-managers and out of the hands of estates.

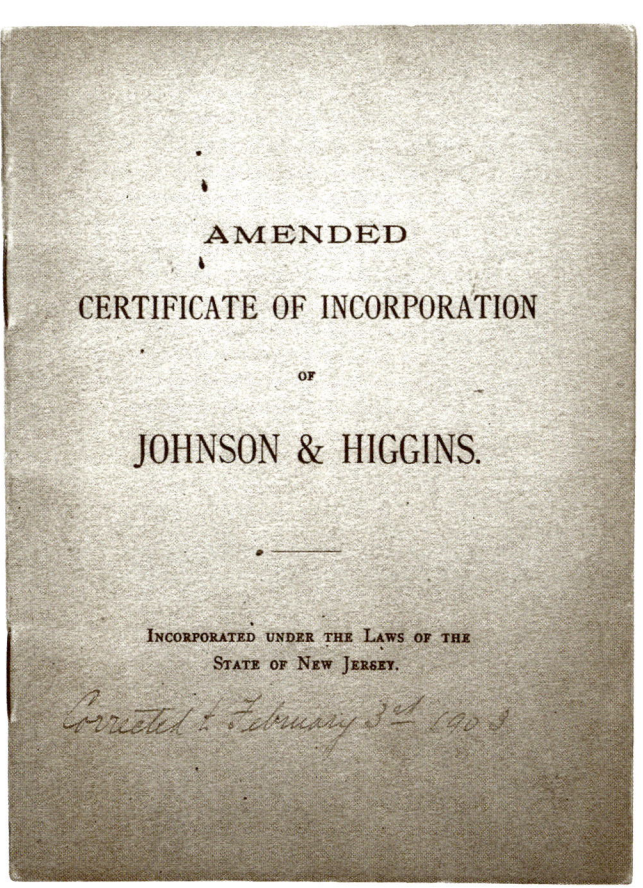

tions, although most professional service firms — including those in insurance brokerage, law, accounting and investment banking — continued as unincorporated partnerships.

However, the right of corporations to own other corporations was hotly contested. In 1899, New Jersey became the first state to make clear that this was permissible, and many companies rushed to incorporate there. The practical effect of the New Jersey rules was to allow corporations within an industry to combine into "trusts," such as the U.S. Steel trust organized by J.P. Morgan and chartered in New Jersey in 1901. In that sense, the incorporation of Johnson & Higgins — which became one of the first companies to apply for a New Jersey charter, even though it had no intention of forming an insurance-brokerage trust — is an odd footnote to history. We are left to wonder what the partners had in mind.

Many of today's major corporations which trace their roots back to this period, including Eastman Kodak, Exxon and Quaker Oats, still have New Jersey charters. So does Johnson & Higgins. New Jersey retained its preferred status until 1913, when overtaken by New York. New York soon gave way to Delaware as the most popular state for incorporation, and of course Delaware retains that position today because of its generally favorable corporate regulations.

Whatever the reasons for incorporating, J&H's partners went about the task with great care: they created a charter and bylaws that, with modifications, still provide a highly effective means for transferring ownership of the firm to new generations of partners. Through this unique mechanism, the company's shares are recycled into the hands of directors who are active in the business and are kept out of the hands of retired directors and estates. Ownership by estates is one of the banes of privately held businesses, often resulting in estate tax problems. In fact, since the 1960s, several large insurance brokerage firms, investment banks and other service companies have been forced to go public to raise money to pay estate taxes. Because of the foresight of its partners in 1899, J&H has never faced this problem.

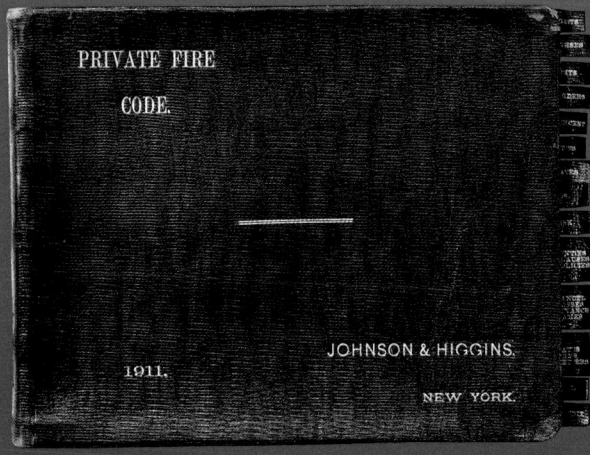

Growth in demand for property insurance was spurred by disasters such as the 1871 Chicago fire, opposite page, and the 1906 San Francisco earthquake, above. Immediately following the San Francisco earthquake, J&H sent Alfred Yates, head of its Fire Claims Department, to the California city, where he remained for six months until all clients' claims had been settled. At left is a private code book, dating from 1911, used to transmit proprietary information by telegraph without risk of data falling into the hands of competitors. Entire concepts could be encoded into a few letters.

The *Queen of the Pacific* was a luckless passenger liner that indirectly brought J&H its first branch office. In 1883, when she became stranded near the mouth of the Columbia River, J&H dispatched an employee to settle a client's loss. The employee liked the West Coast so much that he stayed and opened the J&H San Francisco office. The *Queen* resumed sailing, but five years later was wrecked off the California coast, as shown in the photo below.

San Francisco Becomes the Second Office

Looking back to Johnson & Higgins at the end of the nineteenth century, we can discern two other important developments.

One was the birth of the branch office system. J&H opened its first branch by happenstance. In 1883, an employee named James B. Dickson was sent to the Pacific Coast to settle a client's major loss from the stranding of the passenger steamer *Queen of the Pacific* near the mouth of the Columbia River. Dickson took a liking to the West Coast. He also recognized that the region, with its large maritime industry, offered plentiful opportunities for J&H. He therefore convinced the partners to let him stay and open an office in San Francisco. As that office thrived, Dickson advanced rapidly within the firm, eventually returning to New York and serving as president of J&H from 1902 to 1908.

The success of the San Francisco office sparked a fusillade of expansion. A second branch was opened in Philadelphia two years later, and by 1899 J&H had offices in eight cities across the U.S. This early burst of geographic expansion would not be matched until the 1960s, when J&H would again start adding aggressively to its branch system. Today, J&H has 70 offices in the U.S. and Canada and 50 other offices around the globe.

The second major development was the growth in demand for fire insurance (now called property insurance), kindled by the great 1871 Chicago fire and the Boston conflagration a year later. Johnson & Higgins recognized this opportunity but moved cautiously, preferring to concentrate on marine insurance. By 1901, of the New York office's net earnings from insurance brokerage, $239,000, or 90 percent, came from marine insurance and $25,000 from fire insurance. Although it may have made sense at the time, the firm's reluctance to enter non-marine markets would eventually prove to be a mistake. By the late 1940s, when the marine market began to shrink, J&H was left to play catch-up in non-marine businesses. Today, J&H has overcome that slow start to become a major participant in virtually every area of insurance brokerage.

How Philadelphia Grew

Johnson & Higgins at the turn of the century can be described, in brief, as follows:

- Eight offices
- Six partners
- Seventy-five employees
- Highly profitable
- America's number one firm in marine insurance brokerage and average adjusting
- Small positions in fire and casualty insurance brokerage

The Philadelphia office provides a snapshot portrait of the company as it continued to grow in the early years of the new century. J&H opened the Philadelphia office in 1885 by hiring two local men with superb credentials: John H. Gourlie, Jr., an average adjuster, and William W. Curtin, an insurance broker whose father had been governor of Pennsylvania during the Civil War. The office was successful from the start, providing average adjusting and marine insurance brokerage services to an array of local companies. A fire insurance department was added several years later and a casualty insurance department early in the twentieth century.

One of the colorful characters who joined the office not long after its formative years was Charles Patrick Francis Xavier Cunningham, known affectionately as "Uncle Charlie." Seth Faison, J&H's former manager of corporate communications, remembers Cunningham as "a crusty old guy who was tough as nails, but also had a heart of gold." Cunningham once described himself as a "tough, two-fisted Irishman." Cunningham joined the Philadelphia office in 1913, at a time when new hires were expected to start at the very bottom. College degrees were virtually unheard of within the firm, and indeed within the brokerage industry. (This was not unique to insurance brokerage. Even would-be attorneys didn't have to go to college, but could learn the profession by apprenticing with lawyers.) Before his death, in a 1984 interview with Rod Day, Cunningham said he

was 14 years old when he began at the Philadelphia office as an errand boy at $3 a week, including half a day on Saturday. After a few months, he was promoted to mail boy at $5 a week. His first big break came several months later when he was assigned to the marine brokerage staff. He eventually headed the Philadelphia Marine Department, retiring in 1966 after 53 years with J&H. Cunningham's department became known as a training ground for J&H executives. Among those who worked under him early in their careers were chief-executives-to-be Dorrance Sexton and Richard Purnell. Cunningham loved to joke that Sexton, a Princeton graduate of exceptional intellect, was "the best chauffeur I ever had."

Over the years, the Philadelphia office expanded not only through internal growth, but also through the acquisition of other firms — a point that was true of J&H generally. In 1899, a local broker named William Brockie closed his firm to join the Philadelphia office, bringing with him a substantial book of marine business. (Curtin and Brockie had such fine reputations in Philadelphia that J&H's business in the city was conducted for many years under the name Curtin & Brockie, rather than Johnson & Higgins.) In 1924, J&H acquired Willcox, Peck & Hughes, a large brokerage company with seven branches across the U.S. and Canada. Some of its clients were located in the Philadelphia area, again garnering marine business for the J&H office. And in 1943, a local broker named Earle Baruch joined the office, bringing with him substantial business. Baruch would later become a J&H director and would head the Philadelphia office for more than a decade.

THE BROTHERS COE

Just as the State of Virginia is sometimes called the Mother of Presidents of the United States, so might the City of Philadelphia be dubbed the Mother of Chief Executive Officers of Johnson & Higgins. In addition to Sexton and Purnell, CEOs William Brockie and William LaBoyteaux began their careers in the City of Brotherly Love.

Still further, soon after it opened in 1885, the Philadelphia office hired an astute 16-year-old, W.R. Coe, who had lately migrated from England. Two years later, his younger brother, George, was hired. Both would become major figures in the affairs of J&H during the first four decades of the twentieth century, with W.R. serving as president and chief executive officer from 1910 to 1916. He would also marry into great wealth and thereby become possibly the richest person ever to work at Johnson & Higgins.

W.R. Coe trained as an average adjuster under the tutelage of John Gourlie, the first manager of the Philadelphia office. Coe moved ahead rapidly and in 1893 was transferred to New York, advancing to manager of the New York Adjusting Department seven years later. That same year, 1900, at 31 years of age, he was

J&H president William R. Coe was a leading authority on average adjusting. His 1912 volume, *Law and Practice of General Average in the United States*, was the definitive book of its time on the topic.

J&H conducts its business largely through subsidiaries. This early stock certificate represented ownership of Johnson & Higgins (Maryland) Inc., which operated the Baltimore office.

elected chairman of the Association of Average Adjusters of the United States, the prestigious industry position once held by J&H co-founder Henry Johnson. In 1903, Coe became a J&H director, assuming the presidency seven years after that. The one-time junior clerk was by now a respected authority on average adjusting and in 1912 wrote *Law and Practice of General Average in the United States*, the definitive book of its time on the topic.

Meanwhile, brother George became a successful marine insurance broker, transferring to New York in 1895, two years after W.R. George subsequently advanced to manager of the New York Fire Insurance Department and later of the New York Casualty Department, and was elected a director in 1907. He was known as one of J&H's most accomplished marketers, winning important new clients for the firm.

But as successful as George was, it was W.R. Coe who truly made his mark, becoming a tycoon straight out of central casting. His first wife, Jane, died in childbirth in 1898. Two years later he married Mai Rogers, whose father was one of the founders of Standard Oil. W.R. and

The caption for this 1930 photo says, "Truckload of some of the 1,500 former unemployed men who have been given temporary jobs as apple merchants in accordance with the plan devised by Joseph Sicker, National Chairman of the International Apple Association." Even at the depths of the Depression, J&H cut salaries but did not lay off any employees.

Mai Coe traveled widely and had far-ranging interests, even becoming good friends of the legendary William F. "Buffalo Bill" Cody. When Mai's father died in 1909, she inherited great wealth. In 1910, W.R. and Mai purchased Cody's Wyoming property, developing it into a one-million-acre ranch. Through their association with Cody, they also became interested in Western American history, assembling a major collection of papers and artifacts that would eventually be donated to Yale University. In 1913, back in New York, the Coes purchased the Planting Fields estate and transformed it into one of the great homes on Long Island's fabled north shore.

W.R. Coe withdrew from day-to-day involvement in Johnson & Higgins in 1916 at age 46. However, he continued as chairman of the board, presiding for many years at the J&H annual meeting — much to the annoyance of his successor, CEO William LaBoyteaux. George Coe continued to work full-time, remaining active in the business until 1943, when both brothers retired from the board after nearly six decades of association with the firm.

After W.R. Coe died in 1955 (Mai had passed away three decades earlier), their beloved Planting Fields estate was turned into a museum and public garden that is today a popular Long Island tourist attraction famous for its magnificent azaleas and rhododendron.

1845-1945: ROOTS OF A MODERN FIRM

THE GREAT DEPRESSION

When the Great Depression of the 1930s swept across the American landscape like a twister across the plains, leaving many businesses in shambles, J&H suffered less damage than many others. Costs were trimmed by the closing of offices in Baltimore, Boston and New Orleans. Employees were bade, when traveling on business, to book lower berths (which were less expensive than staterooms), to "avoid taxis" and instead "use street cars and buses," and to "tip with discretion." The firm also decreed that entertaining "must be curtailed." More significantly, J&H imposed an across-the-board pay cut of

W.H. LaBoyteaux loved to send missives to employees, expounding his views on how they should conduct themselves to assure J&H's continued success.

ESTABLISHED 1845

INCORPORATED 1899

CABLE ADDRESSES:

BALTIMORE — AVEJUSTER
BOSTON — AVERAGIUM
BUFFALO — TUNEDEPTH
CHICAGO — CHIKERODEN
CLEVELAND — TUNEDEPTH
DETROIT — DETHERODEN
LOS ANGELES — ANGKERODEN
NEW ORLEANS
  (ADJUSTING) — AVSTATER
  (BROKERAGE) — TUNEDEPTH
PHILADELPHIA — NITRUG
SAN FRANCISCO — ADJUSTER
SEATTLE — AVERAGE
HAVANA — HAVKERODEN
MONTREAL — AVARIE
VANCOUVER — TUNEDEPTH
WINNIPEG — WINKERODEN

JOHNSON & HIGGINS
WILLCOX, PECK & HUGHES, INC.
AVERAGE ADJUSTERS & INSURANCE BROKERS

MARINE
PROTECTION & INDEMNITY
FIRE - AUTOMOBILE
LIABILITY - COMPENSATION
SURETY BONDS
CASUALTY
GROUP
LIFE

67 WALL ST.
CABLE ADDRESSES "KERODEN" "TUNEDEPTH"

NEW YORK, May 11, 1933.

PLEASE ADDRESS REPLY TO
MARINE DEPARTMENT
FOR ATTENTION OF W. H. LaBoyteaux

Fellow Employees of Johnson & Higgins:

    The message of our President to the country over the radio on Sunday evening last, has inspired this communication to each and every member of the staff, from the highest to the lowest.

    The past three years have had many difficulties, many setbacks, and discouragements for all. I doubt that there is one single person in the entire country who has not been adversely affected.

    During these difficult times, the organization of Johnson & Higgins, from the home office to the smallest of its branch offices, has carried on with courage and cooperation. Sustained effort, efficiency, and cooperation are the bulwarks of any enterprise.

    The President's talk should give us renewed confidence and courage for the future; but no sustained improvement can be expected unless each of us will put his shoulder to the wheel and, by hard work and undiminished effort, do his utmost to help in that most desirable end.

> "There is a tide in the affairs of men which
> Taken at its flood, leads on to fortune."
>   Shakespeare.

    In my personal opinion, that turn of the tide is now at hand.

    I am, therefore, addressing each of you to thank you for your past loyalty to the organization, and your individual and collective efforts in maintaining our esprit de corps and our standards of service to our clients.

    I wish to add that with a continuation of this same spirit and the increase in our efforts, which the encouragement of a better future outlook should give us, I am confidently looking forward to bigger and better things for us in the future that lies before us.

Very sincerely yours,

W. H. LA BOYTEAUX

10 percent followed by another of 20 percent. However, the directors absorbed all losses beyond the amount of the pay cuts, so that no one had to be laid off, and by 1936 pay had been restored to its pre-Depression levels. Nonetheless, some of the directors continued to feel a pinch. Each director received an annual draw of $10,000 plus a year-end check for his share of the profits. It was said that when H.H. "June" Salmon, Jr., was elected to the board at the beginning of 1939, his share of earnings fell short of his draw that first year. At year end, he was astonished to receive a bill instead of a check.

Throughout the Depression, Johnson & Higgins people were generous in helping others less fortunate than themselves. Responding to the appeals of the Emergency Unemployment Relief Committee, established in 1930 to assist those out of work, every employee of J&H made a contribution, averaging about two percent of salary.

Even at the depths of the Depression, J&H did some hiring, although each staff addition had to be approved personally by CEO LaBoyteaux. One recruit was David Winton, who would go on to head the Casualty Department and become one of the more memorable individuals in J&H history, a renaissance man with interests ranging from literature to motorcycles to flying. Winton had attended Princeton University for two years, but was forced to drop out due to family financial problems. He worked one year at a small insurance agency before joining J&H in 1935 at $18 a week. Early-on, he was told by a mentor that it was good for the industry, for one's employer and for one's own career to donate time to trade groups and other industry activities. He would follow this advice religiously, and as he moved up the corporate ladder would pass it on to younger associates.

Tall, trim and distinguished looking, Winton retired in 1979. In an interview not long ago, he described the first big break of his career. In 1940, Johnson & Higgins, which was very low-key about promoting itself, was approached by Doremus & Company, an advertising agency, which suggested a coast-to-coast advertising campaign. LaBoyteaux, the J&H president, was skeptical, believing the name of Johnson & Higgins was so well

known in the business community that there was no need to advertise. The Doremus representatives thereupon suggested that a simple questionnaire be sent to the chief executives of corporations across the U.S. asking what they knew about J&H. "The answers [to that

J&H launched its first national advertising campaign in the early 1940s. President W.H. LaBoyteaux agreed to advertise only after a survey showed that many business executives thought J&H was a stock broker.

questionnaire] changed the shape and life of Johnson & Higgins as quickly as anything else that ever happened to the firm in nearly 100 years!," Winton wrote in his 1987 book, *Recollections of Johnson & Higgins: 1935-1979*. To LaBoyteaux's shock and dismay, the overwhelming majority of the replies were "don't know" or "stock and bond brokers." It was rumored that Doremus had agreed to pay for the mailing if more than 50 percent of the respondents knew about J&H, while LaBoyteaux had agreed that J&H would pay if fewer than 50 percent were familiar with the firm — and, of course, LaBoyteaux lost.

Immediately, there was a flurry of activity to prepare an advertising campaign, the first in J&H history and one of the first in the brokerage industry. Concurrently, LaBoyteaux agreed that J&H should sponsor an essay contest among its employees, asking them to write something pertinent about the firm or the role of the insurance broker. These essays, it was thought, might provide ideas for J&H's advertisements. Winton was still a junior employee in the Casualty Department and felt compelled to take part in the essay contest, believing it might aid his career. All told, 151 papers were submitted — and Winton's was the winner. His essay, titled "Does Mutual Insurance Cost Less?," argued for the role of the broker and said, in part, "The story of ourselves and our profession is a story that will lend itself admirably to the simplicity of good salesmanship. For it is basically but the simple truth that proper representation in the purchase of any product or service will ultimately be productive of the lowest cost compatible with complete satisfaction from the purchaser's viewpoint."

Winton, who was earning $5,000 a year at the time, welcomed not only the attention that winning the contest brought him but also the hard cash that came with it. Just weeks earlier, his wife had given birth prematurely to twins, and the medical bills were staggering. "On the day the contest winner was announced, I was in debt for about $2,000," he recalls. "The $500 first prize knocked off a quarter of that debt in one stroke, and I was mighty glad to have it."

THE ROLE OF THE BROKER

In 1945, Johnson & Higgins marked the 100th year of its founding and, as part of the celebration, published a book summarizing its first century. That book asked the most pertinent question of all: What is the role of the insurance broker and why should companies use one? The question remains as timely as ever today.

The 100th anniversary book answered the question by outlining the role of the broker as follows:

1. Seek out underwriters and secure the best terms and conditions possible in behalf of clients.
2. Make certain the underwriter is responsible.
3. Collect and assure payment of premiums.
4. Assist the insured in the event of loss.
5. Assist the insured with advice which will prevent or reduce the risk of loss and thereby reduce the cost of insurance.

Today, the role of the broker is far more complex. "Historically, our most important role was to seek out underwriters and secure the best terms and conditions, collect the premium and all that — in other words, the transaction part of the business," says Richard A. Nielsen, J&H president and chief operating officer. "In my view and I think in our clients' view, that is the least important role we play today. It is clearly still part of our job. But the advice and counsel and the other things we bring to the table are, I believe, so much more highly valued by clients than the transaction alone. Plenty of buyers say, 'Any broker can get me $100 million of umbrella coverage,' or whatever the request is. 'What I need is astute advice.'"

An essential point, however, remains unchanged: the broker represents the buyer of insurance, not the seller, and as such can make a vital contribution to a client company's success.

In 1945, at 100 years, Johnson & Higgins was successful and highly respected. The foundations for today's J&H were in place.

ONE HUNDREDTH ANNIVERSARY
JOHNSON & HIGGINS, N.Y.
PLAZA HOTEL — NEW YORK CITY
JANUARY 20, 1945

In 1945, Johnson & Higgins celebrated its 100th anniversary with a gala dinner at New York's famed Plaza Hotel.

3.

W.H. LaBoyteaux: Tough-Minded Boss

William Harvell LaBoyteaux was a controversial, bigger-than-life figure who ruled Johnson & Higgins with an iron hand for 31 years — from 1916 until his death in 1947. His tenure marked the end of an era: the last great period when marine brokerage dominated the firm and the last era of authoritarian leadership by one man.

Known as "Bill" to senior partners and "Harvell" to his closest friends, the diminutive, distinguished-looking LaBoyteaux was the leading authority of his time on ocean marine insurance. Charles Page, a J&H director from 1944 to 1964, knew LaBoyteaux for more than 30 years. He recalls the J&H chief as being "very calm, a twinkle in his eye, always had a good logical presentation of what he wanted to achieve — I can't say enough about his good qualities." On the other hand, LaBoyteaux ran the firm like a fiefdom. He made all decisions by himself, not giving the slightest consideration to the views of his partners. "No votes taken," in the words of Page.

LaBoyteaux was born in Henderson, North Carolina, in 1872 and journeyed to New York at age 17 to work as a clerk at an average adjusting firm. He soon transferred to Philadelphia and subsequently joined the British and Foreign Marine Insurance Company in that city.

With his work ethic and incisive mind, he was a young man on a fast track. In 1894, only 22 years old, he was hired by Johnson & Higgins in the dual job of average adjuster and manager of the Philadelphia office. Five years later, he was sent to San Francisco, where he would head the J&H office for nearly two decades. It was in San Francisco that he made his mark. According to Page, when LaBoyteaux arrived in the city, "He was very shy about approaching new clients, but he got over that and built a highly successful office." In 1905, LaBoyteaux was elected a J&H director, becoming the only non-New York board member at that time. J&H shares were allocated among the directors based on various factors, including contribution to results. By 1910, LaBoyteaux owned 9.5 percent of the company's stock, second among the 14 directors only to the 10.4 percent owned by president W.R. Coe. LaBoyteaux ended up serving on the J&H board for 42 years, the longest tenure in the firm's history.

In San Francisco, LaBoyteaux lunched alone each day at the city's leading business club, located in the Fairmont Hotel. Reading a newspaper while he ate, he looked up every so often to survey the room. Although LaBoyteaux considered it unbecoming to solicit business, he had no qualms about wooing clients indirectly. Upon finishing lunch, he would invariably "table hop," chatting with clients, would-be clients and others. In this way, he got to know the leaders of the local business community and brought visibility to J&H. After he moved to New York, he joined India House, a club popular with many in the maritime industry. "Exactly the same performance," according to Page, "eating by himself, and that brain would be working all through lunch."

Dispute Over the Presidency

There are various versions as to how LaBoyteaux was chosen to be president of J&H. When W.R. Coe announced in 1916 that he was resigning, there was no clear successor. Dixon W. Kelley, who joined J&H in 1942, heard the following account of what happened next: LaBoyteaux was invited from San Francisco to New York to be interviewed as a candidate for the job. However, stopping on route in Chicago, LaBoyteaux phoned Coe and demanded that he be named president immediately, saying he would not continue to New York unless he was. After a heated discussion, Coe gave in. While Page agrees there was some kind of dispute, he believes LaBoyteaux was in fact offered the job, but agreed to accept it only after exacting a promise that he would have absolute authority.

As president, LaBoyteaux maintained J&H's dominant position in ocean marine brokerage and average adjusting, but overlooked opportunities to expand in other businesses, such as reinsurance brokerage. He was highly respected in the maritime industry for his knowledge and integrity. He was also very firm in his business policies, giving ground to no one. During the Depression, when some competitors began reducing their commission rates, LaBoyteaux refused to do so even though many other J&H directors worried that this policy would cost J&H business. One time, Eric Ord, a director in San Francisco, cabled LaBoyteaux that a major West Coast client was threatening to leave J&H unless the commission rate was cut in half. Ord felt he had no choice except to comply. LaBoyteaux's return cable was swift and unequivocal: "Under no circumstances are you to agree to handle this or any other business except upon our full brokerage basis." He followed with a note, addressed "My Dear Ord," in which he declared, "We are not supplicants. We are intelligent business men with as much dignity and right as the people we serve. We give value for what we get and I see no occasion for being apologetic about the principles on which we conduct our business." In fact, J&H lost few if any clients. Marine brokers were few and far between, and J&H dominated the business, serving virtually all the leading maritime companies, including U.S. Lines, American President Lines and Farrell Lines.

How Employees Felt About LaBoyteaux

LaBoyteaux ran roughshod over his fellow directors. One time, a director had a run-in with a client. LaBoyteaux personally investigated the incident and quickly demoted the director, eventually pushing him

LaBoyteaux the Writer

W.H. LaBoyteaux loved to write, peppering the staff with memos designed to motivate them and share his views on insurance topics. In 1931, he expounded on the role of the "efficient Insurance Broker." Here is an excerpt:

"The efficient Insurance Broker is the ounce of prevention worth a pound of cure.... Forty years ago, the Insurance Broker was a negligible, if not almost unknown quantity in the United States. Most insurance was transacted directly between the merchant or assured with the insurance company or its agents. At that time, when the brokers first became really active, it was predicted by insurers that the broker's life would be short. That he would soon disappear. Today the situation is completely reversed. Practically all insurance is handled by brokers because the need for an expert adviser acting for the buyer as against the seller is generally recognized.

"Some years ago the Cunard Steamship Company, whose executives and directors were also directors on the Boards of several large insurance companies, asked our English correspondents to have one of their partners call upon them. The Company had been placing their insurance directly with the insurance companies with whom they were closely affiliated by representation on their Boards. They asked our correspondents why it was their competitors were getting better terms than they were enjoying. The answer is obvious in the action they later took in appointing our London correspondents their brokers in respect to all of their insurance, which arrangement continues to this day."

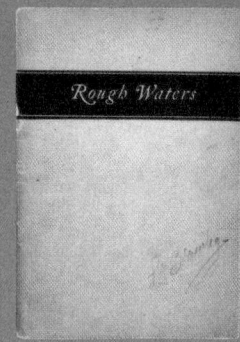

J&H issued an amusing booklet, *Rough Waters*, as part of its 100th anniversary festivities. It was purportedly written by a naive reporter trying to understand the insurance business, although LaBoyteaux himself was most likely the author.

COPYRIGHT 1945—JOHNSON & HIGGINS

PRINTED IN U. S. A.

Foreword

After taking our business rather seriously for 100 years, we decided to celebrate our Centennial by trying to find out whether it had an entertaining side—one which might appeal to the layman. So we engaged an inquiring reporter who knew nothing about insurance brokerage, and asked him to write our story as he saw it. In the following pages you will find the result. It is not exactly what we expected, but perhaps that has its merit. In any event we have published it as written and hope that you may enjoy it. It is presented with our compliments as a souvenir of our 100th Anniversary.

JOHNSON & HIGGINS

W H LaBoyteaux
President

LaBoyteaux wrote three books, including *The Rules of the Road at Sea*, a guide for ship captains.

out of the firm — without saying a word about the matter to other directors or giving them any voice in its resolution. In another instance, when Dorrance Sexton, then an employee in the New York Marine Department, returned from World War II, he asked for a raise from his prewar salary. The salary committee of the board turned him down, whereupon LaBoyteaux summarily vetoed the committee's decision, declaring, "Pay him what he wants."

In 1937, with much ballyhoo, LaBoyteaux established a Junior Advisory Committee, nicknamed the Junior Board of Directors. It consisted of talented younger employees, including Alexander Olsen, Howard F. Quigley, H.H. Salmon, Jr., and John Nelson, who were to advise the J&H board and suggest ideas for developing new business. LaBoyteaux called the program "an experiment which we shall watch with great interest" and told the employees "we are offering you these greater responsibilities to see how you develop under them." At the same time, he established ground rules which some found daunting. He directed that the junior board meet once a month, that it keep written minutes showing who made each motion and that the minutes also state, by name, who voted for and against each proposal. He said he would personally review the minutes and that they would be read aloud to the entire J&H board. After several months of study and debate, the junior board came forth with two recommendations: that J&H establish a separate department for inland marine business and that it offer to handle the personal insurance needs of executives of client corporations. LaBoyteaux rejected both ideas out of hand, saying he didn't see how a separate inland marine department "would accomplish anything that cannot be accomplished now with the present set-up" and that selling insurance to executives had "potential dangers which we would prefer to avoid." Not much more was heard from the junior board.

While LaBoyteaux was abrupt and dictatorial, he also could be thoughtful and considerate, particularly with employees not in positions of authority. "He was a firm administrator, but I never saw anything but a nice man,"

In 1940, J&H moved its headquarters to 63 Wall Street, where it stayed for 30 years. Many long-time employees still have fond memories of the 63 Wall offices, known for their "shabby gentility."

states Alexander "Sandy" Wood, who was a young employee in the New York Adjusting Department when he worked with LaBoyteaux on the firm's 100th anniversary book.

LaBoyteaux had a passion for thoroughbred horses, breeding them at Hop Creek Farms, his 300-acre spread in Rumson, New Jersey. He sold them to others, and even though he was not a gambler and seldom went to the track, he followed the horses' careers with great interest, charting their performances race by race to identify the best bloodlines. It was his custom to invite promising young employees to the farm for the weekend. Such an invitation was invariably viewed by the recipient with mixed emotions. Employees appreciated LaBoyteaux's interest in their careers and looked forward to seeing his beautiful estate, but were terrified they might commit some gaffe that would offend him. "What does he want me for?" was a common response. One of these employees was Dixon Kelley, who worked in the Los Angeles office but was spending a month in New York during the summer of 1945. When Kelley and his wife, Margaret, arrived at Hop Creek Farms, LaBoyteaux laid out a detailed schedule: the wives would have breakfast each morning in bed, the husbands would eat downstairs. Cocktails would be served at 1:15 p.m., followed by lunch. Cocktails would again be served at 6:45 p.m., followed by dinner. "And LaBoyteaux said, 'If you don't want cocktails, don't show up for them,'" Kelley recalls. "Well, imagine not showing up!" The weekend concluded with a black-tie dinner Sunday night attended by members of the LaBoyteaux family, including children and grandchildren. "Even the little kids wore black ties," Kelley says. Monday, back in New York, Kelley lunched at a shabby midtown cafeteria and thought to himself, "What a comedown."

Page says the only time he ever saw LaBoyteaux falter was when the J&H president became overextended in the stock market and did not have enough money to meet his brokers' margin calls early in 1929, before the stock market crash. Despairing that he would be disgraced and have to resign from the firm, he laid out his plight to his good friend William Davey, head of the New York Adjusting Department. Davey mentioned the problem to George Coe, who phoned his wealthy brother W.R. Coe, LaBoyteaux's predecessor. W.R. was still chairman of the J&H board, though no longer active in the business. "W.R. came in from Long Island and agreed to put up the money required by the stockbrokers," Page says, "but on one condition: LaBoyteaux was never to invest in stocks without W.R.'s approval. I think that rankled LaBoyteaux forever."

LaBoyteaux was active in many industry groups. During World War I, he served on a shipping board that advised the federal government. Page says his father, who was chief executive of Fireman's Fund Insurance and headed the government board, always spoke highly of LaBoyteaux and called him "the most helpful, most selfless" member of that group. In 1925, LaBoyteaux helped create the Arbitration Foundation to settle business disputes. And he served in 1943 on a blue-ribbon panel that brought about an historic change in New York State law to allow insurers to write multiple lines of business. He authored three books — two on maritime subjects, *The Rules of the Road at Sea* and *Handbook for Masters*, and one on horses, *Thoroughbred Pedigree Charts*.

In 1947, LaBoyteaux died suddenly of a heart attack at age 74. He had dominated the firm for more than three decades, leading it to growth and profitability in marine insurance brokerage. However, he had shown little interest in non-marine lines of business, had made no provision for management succession and had not made the changes necessary for the firm to prosper after him. Following his death, Johnson & Higgins would go through some tumultuous times before getting back on track in the 1950s.

4.

The Aging Goose With the Golden Eggs

For any company, the key to consistent growth and industry leadership is the ability to change as the needs of customers change. As World War II ended, Johnson & Higgins was in danger of faltering on this count. To be sure, Johnson & Higgins was still a superb firm with prestigious clients. It enjoyed high profit margins and was admired and respected by clients and competitors alike.

However, as Seth Faison observes, "They owned the goose that laid the golden eggs and they thought it would keep laying those eggs forever." Or as Dorrance Sexton said in a 1982 interview, "J&H had stagnated and was living off a fine reputation. Very little was being done to move the firm ahead and overcome inertia." It would take about a decade for Johnson & Higgins to begin to revitalize itself.

J&H AT 100 YEARS

Compared with the snapshot portrait at the turn of the century (see page 41), Johnson & Higgins at the end of World War II can be described, in brief, as follows:

- Fourteen offices in the United States, Canada and Cuba
- Twenty partners
- Five hundred employees
- Still highly profitable
- Still dominant in marine insurance brokerage and average adjusting
- Growing positions in casualty insurance, property insurance, employee benefits and other non-marine businesses

However, J&H's fortunes remained heavily linked to marine brokerage, which accounted for well over half the firm's revenues — and this market was about to dwindle as the American-flag fleet went into a postwar decline. J&H had, meanwhile, been less aggressive than many of its competitors in pursuing opportunities outside the marine business. "Historically, there were two main mistakes," according to Gardner Mundy. "One was our reluctance in the 1930s to get involved in reinsurance brokerage. Another was a reticence to expand our network of offices in the United States. We paused in the process of growth."

Two-Man Contest for the Presidency

On LaBoyteaux's death in 1947, two candidates to replace him emerged. Many of the older partners favored Elmer F. Hunt, a long-time director in the Marine Department, while some of the younger partners preferred Courtlandt Otis, a director in the Casualty Department.

Down-to-earth and well liked, but also a bit rough at the edges, Hunt had joined Johnson & Higgins as a young man and had worked his way up the corporate ladder in the tradition of many of his predecessors. He would spend half a century with Johnson & Higgins before retiring in 1952. Dixon Kelley says of Hunt, "A wonderful man, a great sense of humor. A great four-letter-word man, and I want to tell you he could lay it out."

Courtlandt Otis, the other candidate, had been with Johnson & Higgins seven years. He had owned a casualty brokerage firm, Jones, Otis & Company, which was acquired by J&H in 1940, and was one of the few individuals ever to be granted a board seat immediately on joining Johnson & Higgins. Otis was forceful, capable and dynamic, but some employees also found him abrasive and difficult to get along with. Richard J. Rice, who joined J&H in 1956 and worked under Otis for several years, says, "He looked exactly like Charles Bickford, with white hair, white eyebrows and white eyelashes, and glittering pale blue eyes. He was a thoroughly imposing guy, not one to be crossed. Smart as all get-out and knew everyone in the business."

The contest for the presidency was brief, ending in a most unusual way. The directors were told to cast their votes by a particular Friday, and the results were to be announced the following Monday. Dorrance Sexton, a Hunt supporter, was concerned that Otis might win. Though not yet a director himself, Sexton was highly respected and had considerable influence within the firm. It is said that on Friday afternoon he dropped by the desk of the secretary who was keeping the tally and asked, as if purely out of curiosity, whether all the directors had voted. She pulled out the list and Sexton took a glance, discovering that Otis had won by a single vote. As the story goes (confirmed by Charles Page and others), Sexton thereupon spent the weekend phoning directors trying to reverse the outcome by convincing just one Otis supporter to change his mind. His efforts bore fruit. Monday morning, when the final results were announced, it was now Hunt who had won by a single vote, although we do not know today which director changed his ballot at Sexton's behest. Perhaps this kind of maneuvering was common in that era. Nonetheless, according to Rice, for years afterward Otis felt he had been cheated out of the presidency. Otis stayed with Johnson & Higgins despite his disappointment, later switching from the Casualty Department to become senior partner in the Property Department and remaining one of the most influential members of the board until he retired in 1964.

Elmer Hunt's Five-Year Presidency

Hunt was 62 when he became president. He served for five years, until 1952, in a caretaker role without making major changes in the firm's policies or direction.

One of his priorities was to set an example that directors should step aside at a reasonable age, even though the firm did not then have a retirement policy for directors. By tradition, many directors stayed well into their 70s, stifling opportunities for talented younger employees to advance. According to Kelley, "LaBoyteaux had been president for 31 years, and Hunt said, 'There are going to be no more patriarchs like that in my time. I'm

Johnson & Higgins in Two World Wars

Twice during the twentieth century, when the world was thrown into the turmoil of war, J&H people answered the call.

Nearly 90 employees joined the armed forces during World War I. In addition, as the leading marine broker, J&H played an important role in helping the government insure merchant ships which were at risk of enemy attack. Congress established a Bureau of War Risk Insurance and created a three-man advisory board to help direct its work. William N. Davey, a J&H marine director, was the only broker on the panel.

Approximately one-third of J&H's 500-person staff served in the armed forces during World War II. And again, the company itself was called on to help. After Pearl Harbor, the federal government wanted immediate access to the private insurance market for ocean marine risks it chose not to self-insure. Government officials asked several large brokers to submit proposals as to how they would go about handling this endeavor, and J&H won. The government established a committee of brokers, with J&H as servicing broker doing the actual work of placing coverage for the government.

Approximately one-third of J&H's staff served in the armed forces during World War II, and J&H itself was the government's servicing broker for ocean marine risks. Pictured below are American troops training early in the war.

Loaded Liberty Ship rides at anchor in New York Harbor before joining convoy

U. S. Maritime Commission Photo

"The path to Victory lies across water"

To the victory that now lies ahead, the American ship-owning and American shipbuilding industries have made a major contribution.

To the pre-war American Merchant Marine, devoted 100% to the war effort since Pearl Harbor, the American shipbuilders have performed the industrial miracle of adding hundreds of new ships.

Today America has the greatest merchant fleet in history. May it serve us in peace as it has served us in war.

America is proud of the men who built, the dauntless seamen who have manned, and the American ship-owners who have operated these ships of victory.

On the third anniversary of the completion of the first Liberty Ship, we salute their achievements.

*	*	*

For 99 years Johnson & Higgins have acted as buyers of insurance for leading American ship-owners and leading American shipbuilders.

JOHNSON & HIGGINS
Established 1845

INSURANCE BROKERS

63 WALL STREET • NEW YORK 5

Buyers of Insurance for Commerce and Industry

CHICAGO • DETROIT • PHILADELPHIA • BUFFALO • HAVANA • LOS ANGELES • SAN FRANCISCO • SEATTLE • VANCOUVER • WINNIPEG • TORONTO • MONTREAL

This ad was run in 1944, as America looked forward to victory in World War II. Despite the hopes expressed in the ad, the American merchant marine fell on hard times after the war, forcing J&H to accelerate the development of non-marine business.

staying for a few years, and at that point I hope they're going to make changes in the presidency so that a lot of people will have a chance.'"

As might be expected, Hunt was not the dominant CEO that LaBoyteaux had been. He let department heads run their operations pretty much as they saw fit. As a result, the firm soon evolved into an assemblage of departments led by capable, strong-willed partners who would not abide interference by anyone. The Employee Benefits Department, for instance, was headed by Morton M. Denker. "He was a holy terror, so bombastic, so loud," says Edwin L. Knetzger, Jr., who joined the department in the late 1950s after 11 years with the Prudential Insurance Company of America. Knetzger later became J&H president. "I was warned when I accepted Mort's offer that I was moving into the toughest job in the benefits field in New York," Knetzger says. "And I wondered a number of times in the first three months whether I had made a terrible mistake. But happily I ended up getting along well with him. He was so smart, so quick, but so impatient with people. He was the first powerhouse in the employee benefits business, and the growth of the benefits operation at Johnson & Higgins was attributable more to him than to any other human being." Roby Harrington, Jr., who led the Property Department for many years, was another of the directors who would not tolerate interference by anyone in his department's operations.

Many long-time J&H employees look back fondly to this period in the firm's history, when the company was still small enough for everyone to know everyone else and was still riding the crest of its glory years in the marine business. Even today, Dickinson C. Ross remembers being hired by the Los Angeles office in 1953 and being told by John S. Wiester, the branch manager, that working for J&H was an "honor." (There are, of course, many people at J&H who share that pride today, although they might not use the same word.) A graduate of the University of Southern California, Ross had been a movie actor, playing the juvenile lead in the 1948 film, "Good Sam," starring Gary Cooper and Ann Sheridan. After the movie studio chose not to renew his contract, he decided to go into the insurance business. At Johnson & Higgins, he quickly came to love the camaraderie and the commitment to excellence — and had to agree with Wiester's assessment. Ross eventually succeeded Wiester as head of the Los Angeles office and with co-manager E. Eric Johnson helped build it into the dominant insurance broker in Southern California. He retired in 1985.

Matthew Gormley joined the New York Marine Department in 1953. A graduate of Holy Cross College in Worcester, Massachusetts, he had just completed a tour of duty in the navy and was looking for a job when a family friend told his mother that J&H might be hiring. "I didn't have any idea what Johnson & Higgins was, never heard of it," he recalls. He arranged to see Howard Quigley, one of the directors in New York. On arriving at the J&H office, Gormley says, "I talked with him for five minutes. Then he sent me in to see 'Pop' Anderson, another director. I talked with him for maybe one minute. That was on a Wednesday, and on Friday they called and asked if I would start on Monday. It was so nonchalant." Gormley adds, "I liked it the day I walked in the door." He cites the friendliness of the people and the way they cared about each other.

At that time, Johnson & Higgins was experiencing its first great influx of college graduates, especially from Princeton. Dorrance Sexton had joined J&H out of Princeton in 1933, and other Princeton grads followed — including Dick Henshaw, Dick Purnell, Tommy Chester, Dick Mittnacht, Harvey Kelsey, Ward Chase, Mitch LaMotte, Ed Knetzger and Joe Roxe, all of whom went on to become J&H directors. It is now many years since J&H was known as a Princeton firm. Old school ties no longer count much in any business. Today, Johnson & Higgins employs graduates of colleges and universities all across the nation and, indeed, around the world. CEO David Olsen is a graduate of Bowdoin College in Maine and President Dick Nielsen attended the University of Miami and the Wharton School of the University of Pennsylvania.

Until the late 1930s, employees were notified of salary increases by means of little cards, about the size of business cards, inserted in envelopes and placed on the employees' desks. Here are some of the cards received by Alexander Olsen, who joined the New York Cargo Department in 1916 and got his first raise to $10 a week the following year. By 1936, he was making $5,000 annually.

Conservative Demeanor

Despite the arrival of young men with fresh ideas, throughout the postwar era the firm remained rooted in customs of the past. This point was not unique to Johnson & Higgins. Virtually all service companies — including law firms, advertising agencies and investment banking houses, as well as insurance brokerage firms — remained insular in their practices until the 1960s or 1970s, when competition began to sweep through the service industry. On the other hand, perhaps there was a certain charm in the fact that all men who worked for J&H were expected to wear hats with their business suits. It was certainly a time of less intense day-to-day pressure and more genteel manners than we know today, and who is to say which era is better?

In 1939, Sandy Wood, newly graduated from Princeton, joined Johnson & Higgins as an office boy in the New York Adjusting Department. He was required to wear a Chesterfield coat and a homburg when delivering documents to insurance companies in lower Manhattan. "One day I was eating a banana, dressed in my Chesterfield and homburg, when I rounded the corner and ran right into J.P. Nelson, who headed the Adjusting Department," Wood recalls. "He bawled me out right there on the street and then demanded to see me when I got back to the office and bawled me out again. He said, 'Johnson & Higgins employees do not eat bananas on the street.'"

Another time, a well-liked director named John S. Keegan caught Wood whistling in the office hall. Wood recalls, "I said, 'Gee, Mr. Keegan, I guess I always whistle when I'm happy.' He took me into his office and said, 'I'm glad you're happy, but please don't whistle in the hall again.'"

On the other hand, Wood tells a remarkable story about the integrity of reputable firms in the insurance business. During the 1940s, J&H employees still worked a half day on Saturday, in addition to Monday through Friday. One Saturday, Wood placed a large volume of marine coverage for clients, obtaining commitments from underwriters by phone. Because he was so busy, he never found time to get the underwriters' signatures, planning to do so on Monday. These events occurred on December 6, 1941. The next day Pearl Harbor was bombed. Hearing the awful news, and being a newcomer to insurance brokerage, Wood assumed the underwriters would never honor their verbal commitments but would insist on charging higher wartime premium rates. He immediately phoned his boss to discuss the problem, but the boss told Wood not to worry, that an underwriter's word was as good as any written contract. And, indeed, the underwriters honored, without question or comment, all the commitments they had made on Saturday.

From 1940 to 1970, Johnson & Higgins was headquartered at 63 Wall Street in New York. Although the offices were not air conditioned in the early years, male employees were required to wear suit jackets throughout the day or, if they preferred, company-issued beige office jackets. Kelley recalls, "One day an employee said, 'Oh, the hell with it.' He took off his jacket and there were a lot of oohs and aahs. But he got through the day. They

Regulations
FOR THE
GOVERNMENTS OF THE CLERKS
JOHNSON & HIGGINS
Established 1845

1st.—Clerks must be at their desks to commence business, between APRIL 1st and SEPTEMBER 30th, *not later than 8½ A.M.* Between OCTOBER 1st and MARCH 31st, *not later than 9 A.M.*

2d.—They must not leave their desks temporarily during the day without leaving a substitute to answer for them.

3d.—They must not absent themselves from the office (except in case of illness—and then to advise the officers of the Company as soon as practicable of the cause) without permission of the President or Vice-President being first obtained.

4th.—They must not leave the office before 6 *o'clock, P.M.;* and not then, unless the work in their respective departments is completed.

5th.—Correctness in the performance of their duties is particularly enjoined.

6th.—The affairs of the Company are to be considered as strictly confidential.

7th.—All Records and other Books are to be returned to their proper places by the person last using them.

8th.—*No loud talking, laughing or gossiping* will be permitted.

9th.—One person connected with each of the following desks to remain in the office until the President and Vice-President have left for the night, viz.:—

INSPECTOR'S DESK.	DESK FOR MARKING PREMIUMS.
GENERAL ENDORSEMENTS.	EUROPEAN ENDORSEMENT DESK.
ENDORSEMENT OF VESSELS.	ADJUSTER'S.
BOOK-KEEPER'S.	CASHIER'S.

And two of the Junior Clerks, to attend to any other business that may be required.

10th.—Smoking or the lighting of segars or pipes in the office, at any and all times, is strictly prohibited.

11th.—Each person, upon leaving his desk at the close of business for the day, must see that the gas at his desk is turned off, and will be held responsible therefor. The last person leaving the office at night must put the rooms in charge of the porter.

New York, December 15th, 1862.

In its early years, J&H strictly regulated its employees' work habits, as did most businesses of the time. This notice dates from the Civil War period.

didn't fire him." However, the employee never worked in shirtsleeves again, and neither did anyone else. When the outside temperature exceeded 90 degrees Fahrenheit, the president and the departmental partners would meet, in person or by phone, and usually agree to close the office early.

Gormley says, "In those days the directors ran everything. You were either a director or a clerk. There wasn't any title in between. And in the Marine Department, only directors were allowed to talk with clients. You couldn't run a business that way today." In point of fact, director and clerk were the only titles until the late 1930s — "low-priced clerks, medium-priced clerks and high-priced clerks," in the words of David Winton. Courtlandt Otis introduced the title of account executive to the Casualty Department in 1940, but the Marine Department, where Gormley worked, did not make this change until much later. In the early 1950s, Ward Chase, Roby Harrington, Dixon Kelley and a few others became vice presidents, the first in Johnson & Higgins history.

Even as authority within the firm began to spread to more people with the appointment of vice presidents, geographically it remained concentrated in New York. For instance, branch offices were not permitted to have any direct contact with Willis Faber in London. Because Gormley worked in the New York Marine Department, he could communicate with Willis, typically by cable. When he transferred to New Orleans in 1965, he could no longer do so but had to go through George Owens in New York. Then Owens transferred to Los Angeles and Gormley returned to New York, and Gormley could again communicate with Willis but Owens could not. In fact, all cables to J&H, even those addressed to the chairman, came through the New York Marine Department and were read by the marine directors first. "It was crazy," Gormley says. These practices were ended in the 1970s.

Although the branches had little say in company policy, the branch manager was lord of his realm when it came to day-to-day operations. Of course, communications were far less advanced than they are now, and many companies, not just J&H, allowed their branch managers wide latitude. Many J&H branch managers ran highly successful operations, but were known for authoritarian management styles that might be considered suffocating today. Dick Ross affectionately describes Jack Wiester, who headed the Johnson & Higgins Los Angeles branch from 1945 to 1968, as "a wonderful little Napoleon." One time an employee arrived at the office on a Saturday in casual attire to catch up on work. (This was after Saturday hours were eliminated from the regular work week in the early 1950s.) Wiester happened to be there also — and sent the fellow home to change into a suit. Charles W. Curland, now retired from the Los Angeles office, says, "Wiester's results were good for their day. He delivered what was required. But in today's environment a Jack Wiester would not succeed. On the other hand, he might have adapted. Who knows?"

William E. Hall, the long-time branch manager in Chicago, was equally unyielding. Says Walter E. Klepp, "It was a tight ship. He brought in a lot of big accounts, like Goodyear and General Motors, and you knew he was boss." When Sandy Wood was transferred from New York to Chicago in the late 1940s, he asked Hall for permission to make some sales calls — to which Hall replied, "Son, Johnson & Higgins does not have to ring doorbells."

When Dick Purnell, J&H chief executive from 1972 to 1981, joined the company in the Philadelphia office in 1946, he heard that employees in New York were not allowed to solicit new business until they had been with Johnson & Higgins for 10 years. "Aggressive people may have found it not too easy to stay," he quips.

THE PROGRESSIVE SIDE OF J&H

And yet, despite all this, Johnson & Higgins was successful. It never lost its focus on the client, and many young employees found it an exciting and challenging place to work regardless of the autocratic styles of many of the firm's senior managers. Especially for those who

Established 1845 Incorporated 1899

On the fourth of May, 1940 we will
MOVE
our New York office to
63 Wall Street
Our telephone number, Whitehall 4-3160, will remain unchanged.

Johnson & Higgins
Average Adjusters & Insurance Brokers

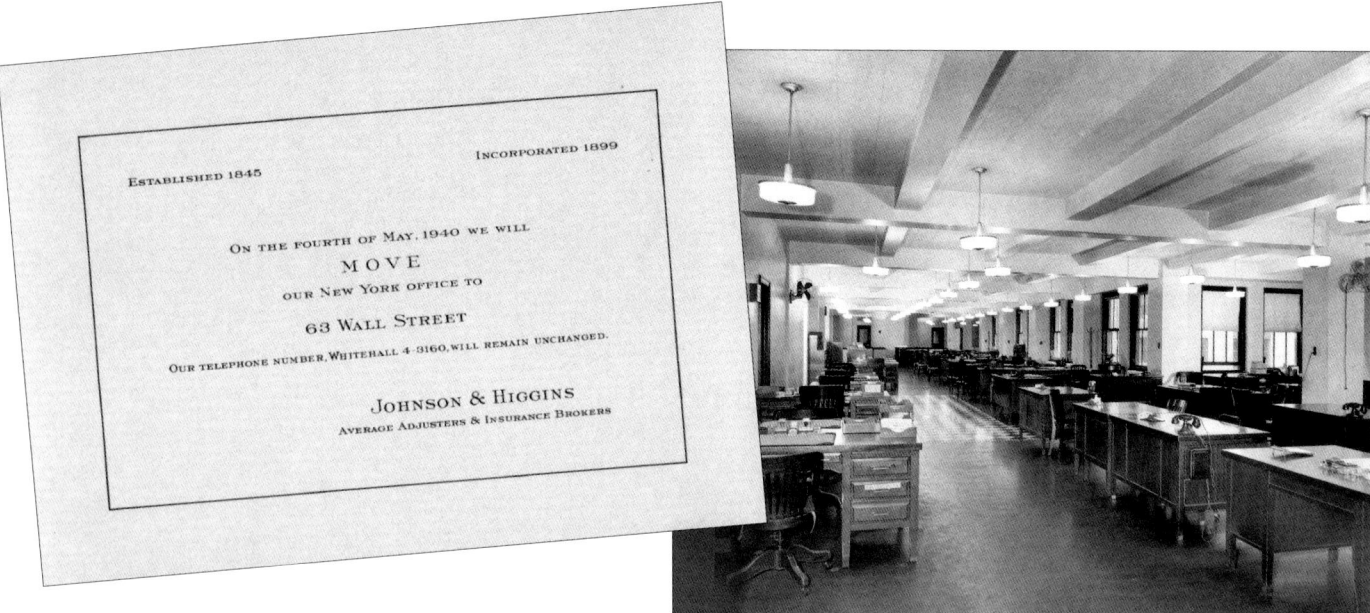

The interior of 63 Wall (see exterior photo on page 54) featured long rows of wooden desks. Conference rooms were small but nicely appointed. Because the offices were not air conditioned, employees were sometimes dismissed early on summer afternoons when the temperature soared.

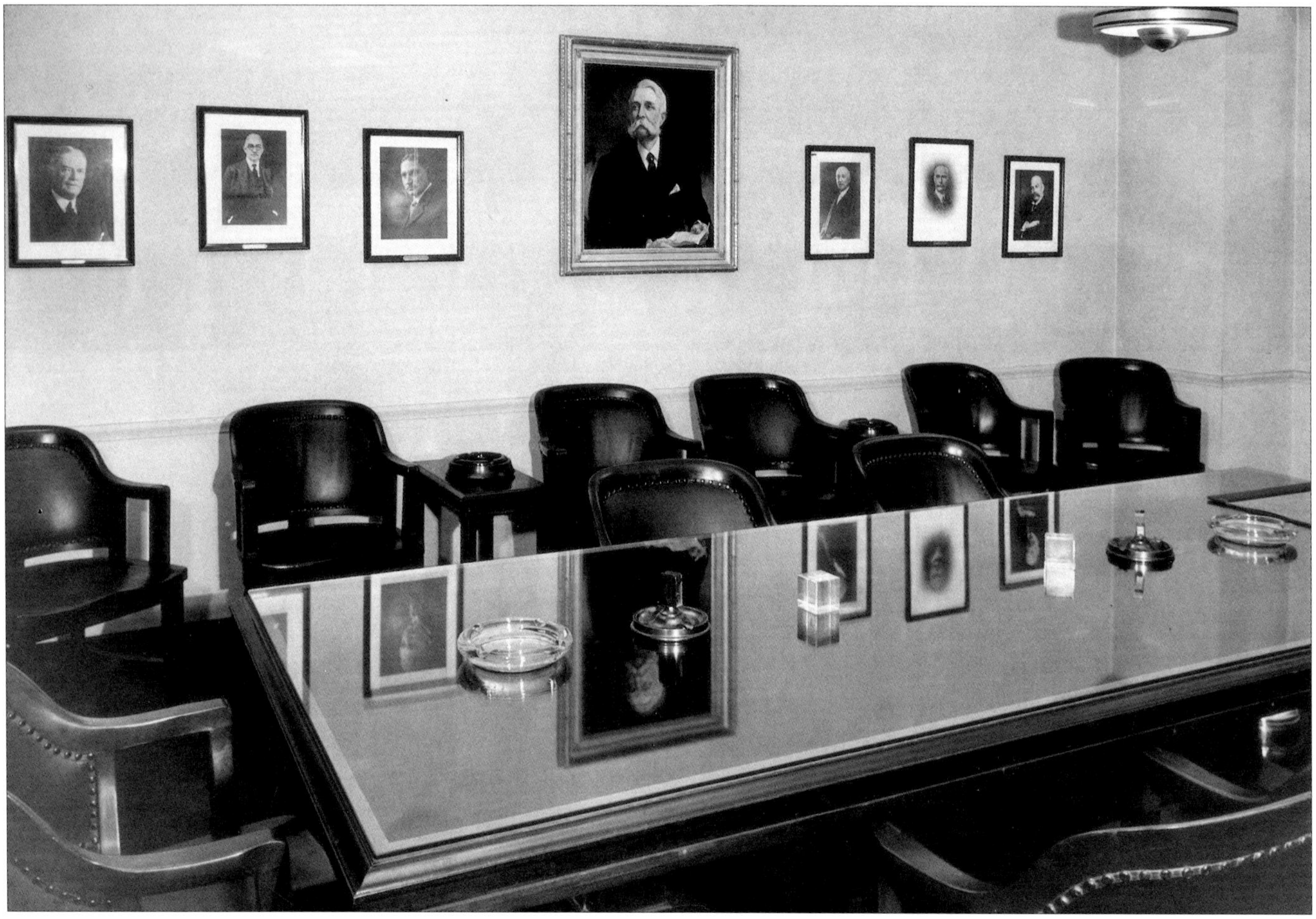

were self-starters and fit in with the firm's culture of teamwork, there was no limit to how far they could advance within the company. Denver Ginsey joined the San Francisco Employee Benefits Department in 1954. The first week he was given absolutely nothing to do. In frustration, he went to his boss and obtained all the reference material available on employee benefits and read it — and read it again. "Pretty soon guys would see me and they would ask, 'What do you do on such and such a case? What are the IRS regulations on that?,'" Ginsey relates. He then put together a list of prospects and made cold calls, landing nearly a dozen new clients. He advanced quickly, becoming a director in 1972, and headed the Seattle office for many years.

John P. Keyser was hired by the New York Property Department in 1965. He says, "Because nobody gave me anything to do, I was scared to death and went out and started to sell immediately. And I used the full resources of the firm. No matter what department or office someone was in, they cooperated spontaneously. They didn't cooperate because the senior people told them to cooperate. They genuinely liked one another and did it because it was part of the culture of the firm." He adds, "The teamwork was always there. We just talk about it more today." Keyser is now a director and manager of the Chicago office.

Matt Gormley, who had joined J&H in 1953, helped open the New Orleans office in the 1960s and developed a specialty of broking insurance for offshore oil rigs, which were just then starting to dot the Gulf of Mexico. It became a sizable business for J&H, winning him recognition and regular promotions. One time, a client suffered the loss of an offshore rig in a storm. Gormley didn't have the technical skill to adjust the claim, so he called the head of the Adjusting Department in New York and asked for help. "He was on a plane the next day," Gormley reports. "The cooperation was tremendous."

The years after World War II also saw the beginnings of one of the major developments in the history of Johnson & Higgins. Immediately after the war, J&H hired its first safety engineers to help clients reduce their insurance costs by identifying and controlling potential losses. This led to the development of a wide array of technical capabilities. Today, loss control specialists and other technical experts are an integral part of the firm's ability to serve its clients.

Moreover, all through this period, Johnson & Higgins never lost sight of the fact that integrity is the cornerstone of insurance brokerage. Dick Ross tells the story of a J&H broker who strayed once — which was once too often — in the 1950s. The broker, who worked in the Los Angeles office, sold a crop insurance policy to a client in Arizona. The broker manuscripted the policy himself, as was common practice, rather than using a standard industry form. The client subsequently incurred a quarter-million-dollar loss from a rainstorm, "and the broker, thinking he was doing the client a favor, changed the contract in Johnson & Higgins' files to cover that damage," according to Ross. The broker thereupon convinced the underwriter to pay the loss. However, Jack Wiester, the branch manager, suspected there was a discrepancy between the contract in the J&H files and the one sent to the underwriter. He investigated, discovered the changes that had been made and fired the broker on the spot. Wiester then told the insurance company to stop payment and related to the client why the claim could not be paid. It took courage for Wiester to inform a client that an anticipated $250,000 payment would not be forthcoming — and to be frank about the circumstances. But absolute honesty was then, as now, the only way to conduct oneself in a business that is based on trust.

5.

Elmer Jefferson and Dorrance Sexton: Turning Point in the Company's History

Dick Purnell says, "When I went on the board of directors in January 1963, marine still accounted for over half the firm's income. Granted, it was highly profitable. But the marine opportunities were not growing. It was the casualty, the property, the employee benefits and all those other things that were considered marginal by many people at Johnson & Higgins. Our people would go to a company and ask for the marine business and forget about the other lines, which grew immensely in the years to come."

Elmer L. Jefferson and Dorrance Sexton, marine partners themselves, had the wisdom to understand that being the preeminent marine broker was no longer enough. Jefferson was chief executive from 1952 to 1962, when he was succeeded by Sexton, who served until 1972. Despite opposition from some board members, who saw no reason to diversify, they headed the company down the road to become the modern, broadly based firm it is today. Their tenures, especially that of Sexton, marked a turning point in the company's history.

ELMER JEFFERSON: RESTORING A SENSE OF PARTNERSHIP

Elmer Jefferson was the last of the J&H chief executives to have joined the company in his youth, with relatively little formal education, and to have worked his way up from the bottom. He began in the New York mail room at age 14 and went on to become an average adjuster. Shortly before his 30th birthday, he was transferred to Cleveland, where he headed the J&H branch for six years, returning to New York in 1934. He was elected a director nine years later. In 1952, he was the board's unanimous choice to succeed Hunt as president.

Forthright and articulate, with the ability to express complex ideas in simple language, Jefferson was admired by virtually everyone who knew him. Richard A. Mittnacht, who spent 34 years at J&H, says, "I can't tell you enough about Jeff's patience, the fact that when you walked into his office he listened to what you had to say. Whether it was stupid or not didn't matter. He made you feel important. A very, very calming influence, very low-key."

Charles Page says of Jefferson, "He was beloved, but he also could be very tough. That was necessary to initiate some of the moves he made."

Jefferson began to rein in the partners and bring a sense of unity to the company. "Under Hunt, many of the partners operated almost independently in their own little bailiwicks," Mittnacht states. "When Jeff came in, he made it much more of a true partnership. He had a healing effect. He brought people together and began to cut out the personal fiefdoms."

Jefferson was known for his ability to see both sides of an issue. David Winton says the only "stormy" board meeting during his own 21 years as a director occurred in 1962, shortly before Jefferson retired. Marsh & McLennan had just announced plans to make an initial public offering of stock, sending shock waves through the brokerage industry. At the board meeting, some J&H directors argued that Johnson & Higgins had to become a public company to remain competitive. Others were equally adamant in their view that even talking about the idea would drive J&H toward making a public offering and that public ownership would be a terrible mistake. Jefferson listened carefully to both sides and reached a compromise solution: J&H would hire an investment banking firm to study the matter and make a recommendation. According to Winton, Jefferson

Elmer Jefferson spent his entire career at Johnson & Higgins, joining the company at age 14 and rising to chairman and chief executive officer.

explained, "We simply don't know enough about it. We will only learn over a period of years, but if we should have to do so in the future, we ought to have some sort of road map." The investment bank duly completed its study, recommending that Johnson & Higgins indeed become a public company. By now, however, the passion of the moment had subsided, as perhaps Jefferson knew it would. Virtually all the directors now wanted to stay private, and the report was filed away to gather dust. In this manner, Jefferson defused an issue that threatened to tear the board apart.

Jefferson had the integrity and courage to make tough decisions when they were called for. Unbelievable as it may seem today, until the early 1960s J&H distributed every penny of profit to its directors, not retaining any cash reserves. At year end, branches paid all their earnings to the parent company in New York for distribution to the directors. Some branches even declared earnings they had not yet received. Stripped of cash, the branches often had to borrow money just to meet the January payroll. Ending this practice would mean offending some directors, who would be displeased with receiving smaller year-end distributions. On the other hand, Jefferson recognized that this policy had long since become outdated and could not be continued. Mittnacht says, "Jeff, toward the end of his tenure, after quite a bit of discussion, finally got the blessing of his partners to start setting aside some sort of a modest reserve fund for a rainy day. Jeff started that and each successor has built on it."

Jefferson was not an aggressive, growth-oriented manager. During his regime, the company did open offices in Wilmington, Minneapolis and Atlanta, the first new domestic offices (with the exception of Pittsburgh in 1947) in 30 years. However, rapid expansion on the domestic front would have to wait until the 1970s, when Purnell became CEO.

On the other hand, during Jefferson's tenure J&H launched an extraordinary program of overseas expansion that would literally transform the company, as we shall see in Chapter 6. Jefferson was not the catalyst for this major undertaking. It was led by Sexton, then a partner in the New York Marine Department, with Jefferson's blessing. Everybody in the firm recognized Sexton's brilliance and natural leadership skills, and Jefferson was happy to share the limelight with him. Jefferson and Sexton worked closely together and made a wonderful team. In 1960, at Jefferson's urging, Sexton was elected president, with Jefferson moving up to chairman and retaining the chief executive title.

Taking up a cause that had been espoused by Hunt, Jefferson believed that directors should retire at a reasonable age. In the late 1950s, Johnson & Higgins still did not have a director retirement policy. Lloyd Benedict, who joined the company in 1959, observes, "Many partners didn't want to quit. They kept working as long as they physically could. So Jefferson finally put in a rule that you had to retire at 65, and just to set an example he retired before 65 and let Dorrance take over management of the firm." Or, as Jefferson himself is reputed to have said in 1962 when he opted for early retirement, pointing to Sexton, "There is nothing left for me to do. He's got it all!"

DORRANCE SEXTON: "J&H WAS HIS LIFE, HIS AVOCATION, HIS EVERYTHING."

Dorrance Sexton grew up in a Johnson & Higgins family. His father, Herbert B. Sexton, was a marine director for nearly three decades, from 1920 to 1948. Young Dorrance attended Taft School in Connecticut and went on to Princeton, graduating in 1933. In the spring of his senior year, Dorrance received a phone call from his father saying that Mr. and Mrs. LaBoyteaux and Mr. and Mrs. Cauchois would be dining at the Sexton home that evening, and if Dorrance planned to be home, why didn't he drop in to meet them? W.H. LaBoyteaux was, of course, the president of Johnson & Higgins and Reginald W. Cauchois had just been made a director.

At the time, J&H had a strict policy against hiring relatives of employees, including relatives of directors, but LaBoyteaux was not above bending company rules to suit his own purposes. Dorrance Sexton said later, "I'm

Dorrance Sexton was one of the great J&H chief executives. Intelligent and urbane, he was a natural leader who diversified the company's operations outside the traditional marine brokerage business despite opposition from some marine directors.

sure you can recognize there's no one more assured than a college senior, so I sat down and straightened Mr. LaBoyteaux out on a few things that were worrying me. And in the middle of it he turned to me and said, 'How would you like to come to work for us next year?' Reg Cauchois, I am told, swallowed his coffee cup in the excitement. Well, it meant nothing to me. And I said, 'Well sure,' because in '33 there weren't many jobs being offered."

Sexton would spend his entire business career at J&H, becoming one of its most revered leaders, although his first few months with the company were anything but fun. Charles Page says, "Dorrance was kind of an outcast when he joined the firm. He came in and many people said, 'How has this happened? Why have they hired the son of a director?' Well, Dorrance proved himself by a lot of hard work. He really did. And he gained the respect of a lot of people."

(Olsen notes that Johnson & Higgins' anti-nepotism rules made sense at the time, because the company was a smaller organization and, therefore, it was critical to avoid the slightest appearance of preferential hiring. These rules have since been phased out. "Today, because the firm is larger and there are a great many more women in the workforce, we would lose many valued employees if spouses and other relatives were not allowed to work at J&H," Olsen explains. "We now have more checks and balances to avoid favoritism in hiring and promotion.")

After serving in the navy during World War II, rising to the rank of lieutenant commander, Sexton returned to the New York Marine Cargo Department. He was elected a director in 1949 at age 38, becoming president in 1960 and chief executive officer two years later. He worked throughout his career in New York, except for one brief stint in Detroit in the late 1950s when he was pressed into emergency duty. One afternoon, the entire Detroit staff quit without warning to join a local firm. J&H immediately dispatched employees from New York and Chicago to keep the branch going, including Sexton, who temporarily took charge of the Detroit marine cargo business. On his return to New York, he was given oversight responsibility for the Detroit office and helped shepherd its recovery.

Denver Ginsey says, "Dorrance was a real charmer. He had an air about him that made you just respect the man. He was rather reserved, but not in the least bit stuffy. And he had an incredible presence. Heads turned when he walked into a room." Tall, witty and engaging, Sexton had the sophistication and handsome good looks of a Cary Grant. Many also remember him as a nonstop smoker. Cigarettes were part of his persona. Some friends urged him to cut back, but he never did.

Sexton loved nothing better than dining in a charming bistro or inviting friends to his home for dinner. His wife, Marge, was a gracious hostess. Otherwise, he had few interests outside work. Emil A. Kratovil, who knew Sexton in the navy and later joined J&H at his urging, says, "He had no consuming avocation. He wasn't a sailor. He wasn't a golfer. He wasn't an author. Johnson & Higgins was his life, his avocation, his everything."

When Mittnacht, along with three others, was made a director in 1965, Sexton hosted a dinner for the new partners and their wives at the Pierre Hotel in New York. Mittnacht relates, "He got up and made a little speech. And he said to all the women, 'I just want you to know your husbands have accepted a mistress. Life is not going to be the same for you, because Johnson & Higgins is going to be something in their lives that it's never been before.' He was dedicated to the company and that made the rest of us enthusiastic about working hard and doing a good job."

Sexton loved to travel, spending much of his time visiting J&H offices, correspondents and clients around the world. He understood the value of inspirational leadership. When visiting a J&H branch, he often would stroll from desk to desk and say hello to employees, stopping to chat with them about their work. He also enjoyed being in the company of other business leaders and was admired and respected by many in American industry. Robert V. Hatcher, Jr., who started in the Richmond office and later served as J&H chief executive, says, "Dorrance came down to Richmond one time, and we had a nice party for him. He knew Claiborn Robins of the A.H. Robins Company. Claiborn and Dorrance were two of 20 men whom *Time* magazine had taken on a 12-day trip around the world. Dorrance never forgot that trip. So he came to Richmond, and I got Claiborn and a few other people and we had a wonderful dinner party. I had been with the firm maybe five years, and I said, 'Dorrance, if you wouldn't mind, as we smoke these cigars, these men might like you to tell them something about Johnson & Higgins they don't know.' And in ten minutes he gave them a description of the firm like I had never heard before. This one man, Jimmy Saunders, said, 'I would like to go to work for you, Mr. Sexton, if I were 25 instead of 60.' Dorrance was not a big talker, but when he said something people listened, because you knew what he was going to say would be said right and probably would be important."

Sexton's Growth Strategy

Sexton died in 1987 at age 76. In a 1982 interview with Seth Faison, he looked back on his years as chief executive and explained his goals: "I think without question the major objective we had was to try to move the firm ahead as rapidly as possible, internationally but more important domestically." This decision was propelled in large measure by Marsh & McLennan's public offering in 1962. The prospectus for that offering revealed Marsh's financial results, which showed its revenues were nearly double those of J&H. "This was something of a shock," Sexton said, "and it made us realize if we were going to maintain our competitive position we had to move ahead as rapidly as possible in expanding not only our domestic operations but in providing services that heretofore we had not given too much attention, such as reinsurance."

Sexton began to strengthen Johnson & Higgins' presence in property and casualty brokerage and other non-marine lines. In devising a growth strategy, he knew it would be difficult to compete directly for property and casualty business in the United States, since many large U.S. corporations already had strong domestic relationships with brokers. So he formulated a plan to serve these companies' growing international insurance needs, an area where there was not yet much competition, and use this as a path to gain domestic business. His strategy worked to perfection. Texas Instruments, Chrysler, Johnson & Johnson, Squibb, Warner-Lambert and Gillette — these were just a few of the U.S. corporations that hired J&H initially for international brokerage and then, pleased with the results, assigned at least a portion of their domestic brokerage to J&H as well.

To serve these and other clients, Sexton stepped up the pace of domestic expansion. During his tenure, the firm opened eight new domestic offices, including those in New Orleans, Houston, Portland (Oregon) and Denver. In the 1982 interview, Sexton said, "Almost the last official thing I did before retiring was go to Hartford and open that office."

Dick Henshaw: "The General"

Sexton worked closely with Richard T. Henshaw, Jr., known to many as "The General." Sexton and Henshaw had been classmates and friends at Princeton, where Henshaw was a classics major. During World War II, Henshaw fought in Europe, surviving the Battle of the Bulge and ending his wartime duty as a highly decorated colonel. After the war, he joined the Army Reserve and became a general officer.

The Army Reserve was a part-time commitment. His full-time job after the war was with Johnson & Higgins, which he joined at Sexton's behest. He started in New York, was sent to Detroit in 1960 as branch manager to restore that operation following the employee exodus and returned to New York in 1962 to be second in command to Sexton after Jefferson retired. In 1966, he was elected executive vice president, the first in the firm's history.

Because the two friends were the same age, there was never any thought that Henshaw would succeed Sexton. Instead, he was Sexton's loyal aide who enjoyed the total confidence of the boss. When Sexton traveled, as he often did, Henshaw usually stayed behind to mind the shop. Moreover, all branches reported to Henshaw. He gave the branch managers wide latitude to run their operations. "The old saying was he gave you enough rope to hang yourself," says James D. Altman. "You were out there, and if you made it, fine. If you didn't, you were replaced."

Henshaw was forceful and pragmatic, with a razor-sharp mind. Charlie Binford, who managed the Phoenix office, says of Henshaw, "He had the ability to make things happen, to make transfers work, to motivate people. And he had an unbelievable insight into problems. I wouldn't want to tell you how many times I was sitting in my office saying, 'I've got a big problem here, I guess I'd better call Dick Henshaw,' and have the phone ring and have Dick on the other end say, 'It occurred to me that you might need somebody to talk with in relation to such and such.'"

Henshaw, like Sexton, was tall and imposing. Don Carlson says, "When you saw those two fellows walking down the hall, it was pretty impressive. They were both big men and there was a presence about them. You felt it. Very positive, absolute class."

Sexton retired in 1972 at age 61, reaffirming the principle that directors should leave at a reasonable age, allowing others an opportunity to advance their careers and serve on the board. Henshaw stayed on as executive vice president under the new chief executive, Dick Purnell, providing continuity between administrations. He retired in 1977.

"How Did It Happen?"

Several years after the tempestuous J&H board meeting of 1962, when Elmer Jefferson had ordered the study to determine whether J&H should go public, David Winton wrote a memorandum to himself in which he asked, "How did it happen that with a fifty-year start on most of our major competitors, we occupied a second position in terms of size to Marsh & McLennan?"

In his memo, Winton went on to answer his own question: Because Johnson & Higgins was so dominant from the start in the marine market, other firms chose not to compete head-on. They looked to other areas of insurance brokerage, including property, casualty and reinsurance, and thereby participated more fully than J&H in America's industrial growth. In his memo, Winton recalled that when he joined Johnson & Higgins in 1935, "The Marine Department and its partners utterly controlled the policies, practices and direction of the firm." But this was not entirely bad, in the view of Winton, who for many years headed the Casualty Department, because the marine partners imbued the firm with their philosophy and business ethics. "Marine insurance, by custom and by law," Winton wrote, "relies on the legal doctrine of *uberrimae fidei* [full and honest disclosure, or literally "of the utmost good faith"] in the presentation of risks to underwriters, the handling of claims and intelligence affecting the risk. And so the preoccupation of these men with marine insurance at the turn of the century guaranteed that we would never be the largest firm in the country, but we could always be the best!"

However, in the years since Winton wrote that memo, the competitive positions of the largest brokerage firms have taken an unexpected twist. M&M's going public allowed it to grow very rapidly through acquisition, but most of this growth has been in areas other than retail insurance brokerage. ("Retail," in this context, refers to the full array of basic corporate insurance coverages, in contrast to "wholesale," which refers to placing special and unusual coverages.) Even though Johnson & Higgins has not equaled Marsh's growth in non-retail businesses, it has continued to grow rapidly in retail brokerage even as it has stayed private and has, in fact, increased its share of this key market since 1962. Olsen remarks, "Going public did nothing for their insurance brokerage business or their clients. Since 1962, we have actually grown faster than Marsh in retail brokerage, our core business."

Memories of a Property Insurance Guru

Walter E. Klepp joined J&H's Chicago office in 1944. Over the next 32 years, he gained a reputation as one of the most astute property insurance experts in the firm. Wally retired in 1976 and lives today in Fish Creek, Wisconsin. He talked recently about changes in the property insurance business during his tenure at the company:

"In my early years with J&H, the property insurance companies were a very close-knit fraternity with almost 100 percent adherence to rates and forms promulgated by company-supported bureaus. Our competitive edge relied upon our experts working with these bureaus to obtain lower rates based on improvements in fire protection which we would recommend to our clients. Most other producers did not have such expertise.

"Deductibles were unknown and it was common for huge corporations to file claims for very small losses. Over a period of several years, this ridiculous situation was changed due to pressure from J&H and other brokers. The Insurance Company of North America and Lloyd's started writing catastrophe-type policies with substantial deductibles and negotiated flat premiums. In the 1950s, a series of multi-million-dollar fire losses occurred, and finally most underwriters realized that premiums from large clients should not be used for small, predictable losses. Blanket coverage instead of specific amounts for each location also emerged.

"Manufactured goods, stored or in transit away from the plants, were insured through their own awkward, inadequate methods. These methods became outmoded for large insureds due to the tremendous values and the hundreds of locations involved. Recognizing the need for reform, Baxter Gentry of the Aetna Insurance Company [Gentry later joined J&H and became a director] developed a revolutionary concept called manufacturers output policy which covered on an all-risk basis all goods away from the plants, whether in transit, in warehouses or in stores. A single rate was developed for each type of manufacturer, modified by the loss experience for each individual company. J&H Chicago was very prominent in the development of this concept, and soon most of our large accounts had the benefit of this way of insuring.

"While we were now able to provide all-risk coverage away from manufacturing locations, we could not induce large risk underwriters to go beyond the standard fire and extended coverage. To correct that situation, another innovative coverage was developed known as difference in conditions, which provided insurance for perils over and above fire and extended coverage at the plants.

"Other important developments at that time were captive insurance companies and the tremendous growth of international insurance. Suffice it to say that J&H Chicago was very much involved in both these fields.

"All in all, it was a very exciting era, and gratifying to have participated in the drastically changing property insurance picture."

6.

Going Global

*D*orrance Sexton's decision to expand internationally helped put Johnson & Higgins on the map as a forward-looking firm no longer content to rest on its laurels. J&H got a head start on its competitors in the international arena. Beginning in 1954, when it opened its first office outside North America and Cuba, the company led the brokerage industry in developing an international service capability. Although the decision to go overseas was controversial within the partnership (some directors viewed it as a wasteful diversion of energies and resources), Sexton had the full support of Elmer Jefferson, who was CEO. Asked why he sided with Sexton on the matter, Jefferson is said to have replied, "It's a different basket and maybe some day we'll find some eggs in it." Dick Purnell recalls, "I think the rest of the board thought Dorrance was going on a picnic, but Jeff had a lot of confidence that he was moving in the right direction."

Sexton saw that U.S. corporations were beginning to increase their investments overseas. He realized, as well, that U.S. brokers were ill-equipped to serve the international insurance needs of their clients. This presented an opportunity for J&H.

He perceived also that as U.S. corporations expanded abroad, they were likely to seek greater control of their worldwide insurance programs. Until the early 1960s, most multinational corporations allowed their country managers to handle insurance requirements locally with little or no direction from corporate headquarters. Sexton believed this would change as the financial stakes became higher.

Sexton's commitment to international growth was controversial within the partnership not only because of fears that it might be a costly flop; but, in addition, he angered several of his colleagues by declaring from the very beginning that J&H domestic offices would not share in the commissions paid by their clients to overseas offices. Lloyd Benedict recalls, "Dorrance was adamant. He said, 'Quit worrying about the commissions.' And at various board meetings he said, 'I am not going to cost-account international. International will be very profitable for Johnson & Higgins one day, but it needs time to develop.'"

Initial Focus on South America

J&H's international expansion began in 1954 with the opening of a joint-venture office in Rio de Janeiro. This office was quickly followed by operations in Venezuela, Argentina, Chile and Colombia, giving J&H a lead in the South American brokerage industry which it has never relinquished.

Why did J&H start in Latin America rather than Europe? "The European markets were well developed and highly competitive, and Johnson & Higgins already had correspondents in England, Germany, France and other European countries," says Harry Hollmeyer, who headed J&H's Brazilian operations for three decades. "Dorrance knew it would be very difficult to get going in Europe, and I think he was concerned about offending our correspondents."

Sexton chose Brazil as a starting point when a friend, who had visited that vast country on an economic mission, described its potential in glowing terms. The friend noted that insurance brokers did not exist in Brazil and suggested there might be an opportunity for an American broker to open an office. Sexton jumped on the idea and, at the friend's urging, met with Hollmeyer, a Harvard-educated American expatriate working in Brazil for an insurance company.

Hollmeyer, too, was anxious to give insurance broking in Brazil a try. "Corporations in Brazil were being given run-of-the-mill service by the insurance companies," he insists, "and the insurers were not bothering to find the best rates. There was a good opportunity for a broker to step in and provide value." Hollmeyer quickly signed on to head J&H's fledgling Brazilian operation. Charming, enthusiastic and smart, he built the operation into a powerhouse with offices across the nation. Now in his seventies and retired since 1983, he still lives in Rio and enjoys an active life of international travel. To many J&H veterans, he is one of the great pioneers of the Latin American insurance brokerage industry.

Back in the mid-1950s, travel and communications were still primitive by today's standards. The flight from New York to Rio de Janeiro, on a prop-driven DC-6, took 22 hours with refueling stops along the way. Sexton flew to Rio shortly after the branch opened and made return visits on several occasions. Despite the rigors of overseas travel, international was his baby and he visited the company's overseas outposts as often as he could. Travel arrangements were often made complex by Sexton's insistence that J&H executives never travel together on the same plane in case of a crash. "I traveled with Dorrance, I traveled with Dick Henshaw, I traveled with Dick Purnell, and I never traveled on the same airplane with any of them," Benedict recalls. "It was inconvenient. You can't talk, you can't compare notes, you arrive at different times. But Dorrance insisted on that."

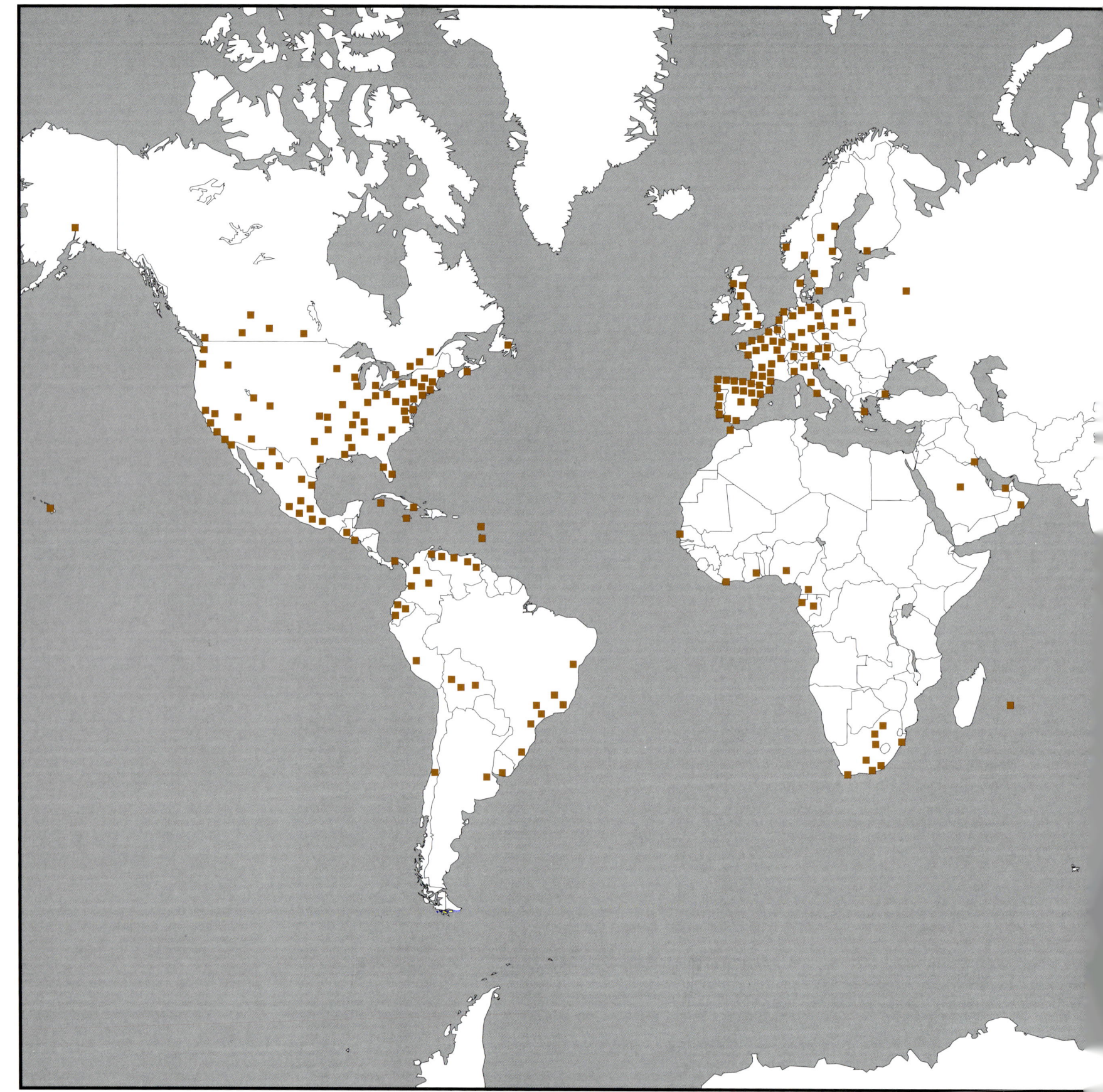

In the 1950s and 1960s, well ahead of its competition, J&H began to diversify globally, initially in South America and then into Europe and Asia.

GOING GLOBAL

BUILDING A BUSINESS IN BRAZIL

Although the main purpose of the Rio branch was to serve the local operations of North American companies, J&H's first three Brazilian clients were, in fact, all indigenous companies — a local yellow pages company, a bottled gas distributor and a petroleum refinery. The refinery was owned by Peixoto de Castro, a wealthy Brazilian lawyer who was stone-deaf. Hollmeyer was introduced to him by Standard Oil Company of New Jersey, a client of J&H in New York. "With their help I made the first of many extraordinary visits to Dr. Peixoto," Hollmeyer says. "He had his secretary at his side, and when he could not read my lips she would repeat and he would lip-read from her, with all of this conducted solely in Portuguese." Peixoto de Castro was a major shareholder in a Brazilian insurance company and found it hard to believe that J&H could beat that company's coverage and rates — a concern raised by many Brazilian prospects in those early years. Insurance brokers were unheard-of in many Latin nations, and there was great skepticism about their merits. "When we submitted our proposal, his insurance company insisted we couldn't implement it," Hollmeyer recollects. "But we did and the refinery was an important client during our most crucial years."

J&H's Brazilian operation broke even that first year and began to generate a healthy profit in its second. Thereafter it grew steadily and, by the early 1980s when Hollmeyer retired, had become J&H's third largest branch in the world, behind New York and Los Angeles.

Another of the J&H pioneers in South America was J. Kenneth Seward, who joined the firm in New York in 1959 and was initially assigned to Colombia. Like Hollmeyer, he ended up spending his entire career in international. Seward spoke recently of some of the changes that took place during his 34 years with J&H: "I saw the business develop from a bunch of entrepreneurs who went overseas and did their own thing. When I went to Colombia, I had to beg to get some money to run the business. And there weren't any coordinated programs. We picked up the 3M account in Colombia.

We sent the information back to our Chicago office and they talked with the risk manager at 3M headquarters in Minneapolis. That might have been the first time he knew about his insurance programs in Colombia. As the risk managers started to get more power and control, they were in a position to develop a Latin American program or an international program. So it all evolved into these global programs we have today."

The 3M Company was just one of many U.S.-based clients that came to J&H through its overseas branches. In fact, Sexton viewed international primarily as a door-opener. Not long after he retired, he said, "International gave us a vehicle whereby we could approach U.S. firms whose business we did not have domestically and talk with them about a service their own broker didn't have. I think really that was the key to those early years."

Don Carlson, who joined J&H in 1960 in Detroit, says, "International was a very special issue that distinguished J&H, and I think we used it well. Stryker Corporation is a perfect example. It was a Marsh account. Stryker was selling products overseas, and I came up with a better idea for handling their products liability coverage. We got their international, and the next thing you knew we had all their business." To this day, Stryker remains a J&H client, now served out of the Grand Rapids office.

CREATING AN INTERNATIONAL DEPARTMENT

Meanwhile, back in New York, J&H decided to develop an international staff. Peter B. Bickett had joined J&H in 1954 in the Property Department, headed by Roby Harrington (known for his quick mind and blustery personality), and was looking for an opportunity to move up the corporate ladder. "One day in 1956," Bickett relates, "Roby Harrington came out of his office and growled, 'Does anybody want to work with Bill Hall [a J&H employee who handled several international accounts]?' I guess I raised my hand faster than anybody else, so I got the job. That was the beginning not only of my international career, but of J&H's International Department because I was the first full-time international employee in the New York office."

Three years later, Lloyd Benedict joined J&H from the American Foreign Insurance Association, becoming the International Department's second employee. Reporting to the office his first day on the job, raring to get started, he was directed to a desk but was not given any instructions or any work. "I was in the office for a few hours," he recalls. "I looked at my desk. I pulled out all the drawers. I dumped all the old paper clips and the lint into the wastebasket. Then an account executive from the Casualty Department dropped by and asked if I would be willing to go uptown with him to the headquarters of Colgate-Palmolive Company. He had been handling the account for years, and the client was interested in meeting someone with international experience." Colgate is a major U.S.-based corporation with operations around the world. Benedict went along, quickly got involved in the Colgate account and never had a dull moment thereafter, as client after client sought his help.

One of his first big assignments was for Chrysler Corporation, which was seeking to standardize the insurance coverages of its manufacturing operations worldwide, a novel idea at the time. "We were able to put together, arguably, the first worldwide, no-coinsurance, single-limit, English-language property and loss-of-profits policy to U.S. standards of coverage," Benedict says. "And the marine boys were able to put together a marine policy covering all the shipments of Chrysler worldwide. And the darn thing worked!"

Continuing to develop its capabilities, in the early 1960s J&H started international departments in many of its U.S. branch offices, the first one being in Chicago under the leadership of Jim Lloyd, followed by Detroit, San Francisco, Philadelphia and others.

ON TO EUROPE

Having established itself in Latin America, J&H turned to Europe in the early 1960s. Sexton was, by now, CEO

By 1966, when J&H ran this ad in *Fortune*, it led the brokerage industry in global expansion with offices and exclusive correspondents in 75 cities.

and, even though his duties had expanded, he kept an active hand in international.

Europe presented an entirely different challenge than South America. Because Europe had an existing brokerage tradition, with many strong firms, Johnson & Higgins decided to compete primarily by using correspondents rather than by opening its own branches. J&H already had a number of correspondent relationships in Europe, some dating back many years. With the exception of Willis Faber in the United Kingdom, all these relationships were non-exclusive.

A crisis arose when Colgate asked Johnson & Higgins and Marsh & McLennan to submit competing proposals for a particular piece of international business — and both firms listed Jauch & Hübener, the premier German broker, as their correspondent in that country. "This was unacceptable to Colgate," Seward says, "and we thus asked Jauch & Hübener to choose either us or Marsh." Jauch & Hübener chose Johnson & Higgins, marking the beginning of a close relationship that continues to this day. Jauch & Hübener's Christian Dahms recently explained why his firm selected J&H: "Marsh had just gone public, and we looked at Frank B. Hall and Alexander & Alexander and thought, 'Well, they may go the same route.' And they sure did. We looked upon the structure of the partnership of Johnson & Higgins and we looked at ourselves and found we were of exactly the same structure. The culture and the philosophy of both firms were so close that, in view of the others going public, we decided in favor of Johnson & Higgins." Jauch & Hübener is today a key member of the UNISON alliance which links Johnson & Higgins and its correspondents worldwide.

Seward notes, "We later developed the concept of exclusivity with all our correspondents, and it stands as a key to our relationships." However, the Jauch & Hübener example notwithstanding, establishing exclusive relationships was not always easy at the outset. On a landmark 1962 trip, Sexton toured Europe with William J. Bumsted, who headed the New York Marine Cargo Department, and Patrick J.T. "Paddy" Stephenson, who was president of Johnson & Higgins (Quebec) Limited.

Stephenson, with his extraordinary credentials — employee of a Lloyd's of London brokerage firm in the late 1930s, highly decorated World War II RAF pilot, wing commander on the personal staff of Lord Mountbatten in the final year of the war and high-ranking NATO official after the war — was invited along because of his many contacts on the Continent and his fluency in French. Paddy was known to speak so rapidly that Sexton once kiddingly observed him to be "fluent in English and French, but unintelligible in either."

Sexton described the whirlwind 1962 tour as follows: "The trip was designed to establish, if possible, exclusive correspondent relationships in the Common Market. In order to cover as much territory as possible, the three of us divided our forces — Bill and I seeing Mees & zoonen and later Jauch & Hübener [the exclusive relationship with that firm having not yet been established], while Paddy renewed his very strong ties in Belgium. I then joined Paddy in Brussels, while Bill went on to Scandinavia. The three of us met again later in Paris to review the French situation."

Relationships with several leading European brokers resulted from contacts established during that 1962 trip, and others were arranged on a second European journey the following year. Was there any resistance on the part of the Europeans to the idea of exclusivity? "I don't recall that at all," Benedict replies. Nonetheless, many of the European firms did proceed cautiously in order to be certain they were making the right decision by aligning themselves with J&H. In 1964, Santiago Gil de Biedma of Gil y Carvajal, S.A., Spain's leading insurance broker, spent an entire week in New York talking with insurance companies, banks and others just to be sure Johnson & Higgins was highly recommended before accepting its proposal.

On their visit to Europe, Sexton, Bumsted and Stephenson came away with the conviction that J&H needed to establish at least one company-owned operation within the European Community as a listening post. Sexton and his colleagues chose Italy because it did not have an existing brokerage structure. The J&H Italian operation began early one April morning in

1964 with the deposit, in a bank in Milan, of the company's basic working capital of $1,000. J&H was the first insurance broker in Italy, and today Johnson & Higgins S.p.A. is the largest retail broker in that Mediterranean nation, with offices in five cities. Its list of clients reads like a "Who's Who" of U.S. multinational corporations' Italian subsidiaries and indigenous Italian companies.

A few of the early correspondent relationships did not work out. J&H parted ways with its French correspondent in 1975 over issues of performance. This proved to be a boon for a major French firm, Gras Savoye, which had been seeking to do business with J&H for several years. "We knew that to keep our French multinational clients we had to be linked, one way or another, to a U.S. broker," says Patrick Lucas, chief executive of Gras Savoye. "The image of Johnson & Higgins in the French market, as a privately owned firm, and their efficiency and power and style, were sufficient. We didn't consider any other firms." Dick Purnell, then chief executive of J&H, didn't want the two firms to negotiate in Paris lest their meetings be discovered by competitors. So negotiations were held in secret in Versailles, and agreement was reached in two days. Like Jauch & Hübener, Gras Savoye is today a cornerstone of UNISON.

Relationships with correspondents in Portugal and Mexico also soured, and the original firms were replaced by others. But no parting of the ways was more startling than that in Japan. J&H's Japanese correspondent was a firm called International Insurance Inc. One morning in 1968, without warning, Sexton received word that the head of International Insurance had been arrested in Tokyo the previous day for pocketing clients' premium payments. "Well, this was somewhat shocking," Sexton recalled later. To fill the void, J&H decided almost immediately to start its own Japanese operation. With the help of Tokio Marine & Fire, a long-time J&H ally, it was able to obtain all regulatory approvals and open its doors within a month. George Rainoff, who speaks Japanese, was chosen to head the new operation, which continues today with offices in Tokyo and Osaka.

How UNISON Evolved

By the mid-1960s, J&H was well on the road to establishing a global network of exclusive correspondents. To discuss common concerns and enable the correspondents to get to know each other, it began holding a series of annual conferences bringing together correspondents from around the world. Many warm personal friendships grew out of these yearly get-togethers, helping to strengthen the ties between firms.

And then the global brokerage business began to change in a way that few had ever anticipated. "Originally we followed our U.S. clients overseas to serve their needs," notes S. Robert Beane, a director in the International Department. In the 1970s and 1980s, however, as foreign corporations began to invest in the United States, the correspondents started introducing their clients to J&H. This "reverse flow" business has added a whole new dimension to J&H's global operations. "We have Japanese business, German business, French business," Beane observes. "We have a flow of business going in many different directions throughout the network, which was something never envisioned by Dorrance Sexton." Or as Patrick Lucas of Gras Savoye puts it, "We probably have 600 U.S. clients of Johnson & Higgins in France. And we have 100 clients from Jauch & Hübener and they have clients from us. And Johnson & Higgins has clients of Gras Savoye not only in the U.S., but in Canada and South America and wherever they are."

At the start, J&H's worldwide network of company offices and exclusive correspondent relationships carried the Johnson & Higgins name. However, with their growing role, some of the correspondents sought a new name that each partner could use to describe its international network. "So we got our heads together," Seward states, "and decided to call ourselves UNISON." UNISON began in Europe in 1982 and has since been extended worldwide. It is not a legal agreement or joint venture, but an alliance based on trust and a mutual commitment to high standards of service. It consists of a dozen partner firms with nearly 15,000 employees in more than 60 countries.

Explaining the value of UNISON to Jauch & Hübener, Dahms says, "UNISON is of very high strategic importance to us since nearly 80 percent of our clients are international corporations. We need international retail services." Only about five percent of Jauch & Hübener's retail revenue comes from UNISON. But Dahms thinks that relatively modest number misses the point. "If we judged the importance of our UNISON relationships on this basis," he maintains, "we would be totally wrong. We have today 120 German clients in the U.S. being serviced by Johnson & Higgins. We would not have our large domestic accounts if we could not provide them with international retail services."

One of the important aspects of international is the exchange of people and cross-fertilization of ideas. Dahms says, "In 1959, even before this exclusivity issue came in, we had the first employee from our firm spend

GOING GLOBAL

UNISON is the global partnership of J&H and its correspondents. Opposite, left to right, David A. Olsen of Johnson & Higgins, Christian Dahms of German UNISON partner Jauch & Hübener and Patrick Lucas of French UNISON partner Gras Savoye. The relationship between J&H and its UNISON partners was strengthened in January 1995 when Dahms, Lucas and Santiago Gil de Biedma of Spanish UNISON partner Gil y Carvajal were elected to the Johnson & Higgins board — the first non-employee directors in J&H history.

a year in New York as a trainee, mainly with Johnson & Higgins but also with the Home Insurance Company. In 1962, we sent the second employee to spend a year with Johnson & Higgins and I spent a year with Johnson & Higgins in 1968-69. Three others have followed. We have always believed in an exchange of people to support the relationship."

In addition, J&H's international operations have been a source of many talented employees for the company. In many instances, these employees have brought fresh ideas to Johnson & Higgins and made an imprint on the firm's culture. Sara Sirotzky is a native of Peru who joined J&H in the Lima office in 1971. Most J&H international offices, including Lima, had active sales programs — unlike J&H in the United States, which tended at that time to be averse to selling. Sirotzky transferred to the Chicago International Department in 1974 and immediately noticed the difference. She kept up her emphasis on sales, and explains with a laugh, "Because I was a foreigner, I didn't know the rules here." Today, she is a senior vice president in the Chicago office, heading a five-person group that sells to and services mid-sized accounts.

Rudi Portaria was born in Shanghai of a Portuguese father and a Swedish mother, was educated in France and China, and joined Johnson & Higgins in Montreal in 1961. "I'm international from the ground up," he declares. He helped open the Milan office in 1964 and subsequently worked in Belgium, ending his career in the International Department in New York. He retired at the end of 1994.

OPPORTUNITIES

Today, all the major brokers have global operations. The competition is intense. Even in the face of this competition, the globalization of Johnson & Higgins, initiated with such passion four decades ago by Dorrance Sexton, has continued. Each of Sexton's successors — Dick Purnell, Bob Hatcher and David Olsen — has recognized the importance of global markets and sustained or

Johnson & Higgins in Canada

Johnson & Higgins has been serving the Canadian business community longer than nearly any other broker. By the late nineteenth century, the company's New York office had already developed a substantial book of Canadian business. In 1906, J&H established an on-site presence by opening an office in Montreal and 14 years later, as its operations continued to grow, formed a Canadian subsidiary, Johnson & Higgins (Canada) Ltd. A second office was opened in 1926, in Winnipeg, to serve grain merchants. Other offices followed, so that Johnson & Higgins Ltd. today has offices in 15 cities from coast to coast.

For a period, J&H operated jointly in Canada with Willis Faber. In the late 1960s, the two firms were looking for opportunities to strengthen their ties by establishing joint ventures around the world. In the first of these ventures, they combined their Canadian operations to form Johnson & Higgins Willis Faber Ltd. However, they severed their relationship in 1991, with J&H acquiring full ownership of the Canadian firm.

Today, Johnson & Higgins Ltd. offers a full range of insurance and benefits consulting services to businesses across Canada.

even accelerated the pace of development. Hatcher, for one, sees global growth as one of the significant accomplishments of his tenure in the 1980s. "In my opinion, those years saw a quickening of our international development," he says. "We really went at it, because I believed the only way for us to accomplish what we wanted to accomplish was by expanding throughout the world."

International operations now account for well over 20 percent of Johnson & Higgins' revenues. J&H is the principal broker or at least involved in the international insurances for nearly three-quarters of the 100 largest *Forbes* companies. Beane says, "I don't think anyone touches us in our international capabilities. It is something our clients know we do best."

Opportunities still abound. For instance, the sweeping economic changes taking place in eastern Europe create a whole new market for insurance brokers. Johnson & Higgins and its UNISON partners are addressing this opportunity as a group. Jauch & Hübener has opened offices in the former East Germany and in Hungary and the Czech and Slovak Republics, regions where Germany has historic ties. In 1993, Gras Savoye acquired the largest broker in Poland, a nation which has traditionally maintained economic relations with France. And since 1993 Johnson & Higgins and Jauch & Hübener have been operating jointly in Russia as J&H UNISON. (Conveniently, the two firms have the same initials, so the Russian name encompasses both companies.)

Another opportunity lies in the development of local business in those countries where J&H has offices, especially in the Pacific Rim. "We see that as a very strong part of our future as we continue to build our international operations," according to Beane. "In Italy, there were no brokers. Now, more than half our business is indigenous Italian business. In Thailand and Malaysia, more than half our business is indigenous. We are involved in large energy projects in Malaysia and the Philippines. When you have privatization around the world and the need for new energy resources, our possibilities for growth are tremendous." Moreover, Johnson & Higgins recently opened an office in Beijing, its first in the People's Republic of China, to serve the needs of foreign investors and indigenous businesses in the world's most populous nation. The office is headed by Alice Tak-Hing Chan, a Hong Kong native who has been with J&H since 1976.

Kenneth A. Hecken, former J&H vice chairman who retired in 1991, sees globalization as one of the single most important issues faced by Johnson & Higgins as the number of clients doing business across national boundaries continues to increase. He believes J&H is already taking important steps to become a global firm, not just an American firm with international operations. The strengthening of ties with correspondents and the development of indigenous business are obvious examples. But he cites others as well, such as the acquisition of equity interests in correspondents in Spain, Portugal, the Netherlands, Sweden and Mexico, the formation with UNISON partners of a Belgian insurance brokerage firm and the revitalization of J&H's worldwide reinsurance business. Hecken also insists that J&H's parting of the ways in 1990 with its long-time British correspondent, Willis Faber, though wrenching at the time (see Chapter 10), was an important step forward as J&H seeks to fulfill its global aspirations. "All the other major brokers are dealing in the U.K. underwriting market through owned facilities," he notes. "We needed to be in the same position."

Ultimately, the challenge for J&H and its UNISON partners is not just to obtain insurance for clients, but to help them manage their risks on a truly global basis — from establishing goals to purchasing insurance or using alternative funding mechanisms, and to tracking coverages and claims worldwide. Johnson & Higgins has come a long way from the time four decades ago when Dorrance Sexton dismayed some of his fellow directors by deciding to open a joint-venture office in Brazil.

In 1968, J&H became the first U.S. insurance broker to open an office in Japan.

J&H now spoken here.

The recent opening of the Tokyo office of Johnson & Higgins of Japan, Inc. is one more step in the expansion of the most comprehensive chain of worldwide insurance brokerage offices. Knowledgeable buyers entrust their international insurance problems to J&H from the Dew Line to Antarctica, and around the world from East to West.

To learn more about how J&H can serve you internationally, write for your copy of our publication, "Corporate International Insurance Programs."

Insurance Brokers—Average Adjusters—Employee Benefit Plan Consultants and Actuaries · 63 Wall Street, N.Y.
One Center Plaza, Boston · 1112 Marine Trust Bldg., Buffalo

Philadelphia • Wilmington • Pittsburgh • Atlanta • New Orleans • Detroit • Chicago • Minneapolis • Los Angeles • San Francisco • Portland • Seattle • Honolulu • Quebec • Montreal • Toronto • Winnipeg
Vancouver • Santiago • Buenos Aires • Rio de Janeiro • São Paulo • Curitiba • Belo Horizonte • Campinas • Caracas • Maracaibo • Puerto La Cruz • Bogota • Cali • Tokyo • Milan • London

7.

Dick Purnell: "My Thought Was To Keep the Momentum Going"

In early 1970, when Dorrance Sexton began contemplating retirement, he laid out guidelines for the selection of a successor. He asked each member of the executive committee to nominate one or more partners, with the stipulation that no one could nominate himself and that any partner over 55 years of age should be considered only if none younger appeared to be ready. Richard I. Purnell, 52, who headed the company's Pennsylvania operations, was the clear favorite and, in fact, was elected. On January 28, 1970, Sexton phoned Purnell in Philadelphia to tell him the news. Purnell remembers the conversation as follows: "Dorrance said, 'I want to congratulate you on being the next president of Johnson & Higgins.' Then there was a thud and he said, 'Are you there?' And I said, 'Boss, I'm not so sure that I am.' I was flabbergasted."

Dick Purnell was a star athlete at Princeton, earning letters in football, hockey and baseball.

In bringing Purnell to New York as president, Sexton wanted to assure an orderly transition. For the next two years, he continued as chairman and CEO, giving Purnell the opportunity to learn about overall corporate matters, such as company policies and worldwide operations. Dick Ross says, "When Dick Purnell took over the reins from Dorrance, he was totally trained and immersed in Johnson & Higgins. He understood everything about it." Sexton gave up the CEO title in early 1972, passing the baton to Purnell, and retired half a year later as chairman.

One of the colorful personalities in J&H history, Purnell is about six feet tall, still athletic and trim in his seventies, neatly groomed, blunt and outspoken, a quick mind, a wry sense of humor, an imposing presence, boundless energy, demanding of himself and others, a stickler for detail, known for his mercurial temper, always ready to admit his mistakes. Ross says, "Tough as nails. Much different than Dorrance. A very effusive personality."

Building on the work of his predecessors, Purnell led J&H through a period of accelerated domestic and international growth. During his tenure, from 1972 to 1981, the number of offices nearly doubled and the number of employees more than doubled. Revenues increased fourfold. Moreover, he helped reshape J&H as a modern corporation. Prior to his tenure, the company had become loose in some of its management practices. Many employees arrived late in the morning, and meetings were often long and unproductive. Purnell would have none of that. He was adamant that meetings start and end on time, that drinking at lunch be curtailed, that phones be answered promptly and that stricter financial policies be imposed to control expenses.

Early Years in Philadelphia

A native of Baltimore, Purnell graduated cum laude from Princeton, where he played football, hockey and baseball. He served in the U.S. Army Air Corps from 1941 to 1946 and moved up the ranks to command the 69th Bomber Squadron, 42nd Bomber Group, in the Pacific Theater.

In 1946, fresh out of the service, he joined J&H as a trainee in the Marine Department of the Claims Division of the Philadelphia office. He still looks back to his initial years in Philadelphia, from 1946 to 1954, with great affection. After the war, he says, "there were still a whole lot of characters in the business, I mean real characters." Two in the Philadelphia office were "Uncle Charlie" Cunningham and "a wonderful old Irishman," Mike McNally, who had been a politician and always wore a derby. Together with the branch manager, Earle E. Baruch, Cunningham and McNally were the office's big producers. Purnell says of Baruch, who was extremely upbeat and personable, "He thought if you couldn't play golf you couldn't sell, and he was a heck of a good golfer."

From Cunningham, Purnell learned the importance of treating underwriters fairly. "If Uncle Charlie didn't make money for his companies, he was very upset," Purnell says. "Although the broker represents the client, if you don't have any companies with which to place the business you won't have too many clients." Purnell also learned the technical side of insurance brokerage and began to solicit new business.

In 1954, he was sent by Baruch to Pittsburgh to manage the J&H office, which was languishing. With characteristic aggressiveness, he quickly turned the business around by bringing in new personnel and landing major new accounts, beginning with the property insurance account of Aluminum Company of America. However, not long after Alcoa came into the fold, two clients left. His spirits low, Purnell phoned Baruch to tell him the bad news. "Earle said, 'Dick, let me tell you one thing. You've lost those. It's behind you. But as head of the office you can't carry a long face, because everybody else is going to become discouraged.'"

In 1962, when Baruch died suddenly, Purnell returned to Philadelphia, taking his place. A few months later he was elected to the J&H board. In Philadelphia, there was an unwritten tradition that competing brokers didn't solicit each others' clients, but Purnell refused to accept the custom and hired a few "young Turks" to land new accounts. One of these newcomers was Rod Day, himself later the Philadelphia branch manager and now a J&H regional director. "Dick's winning attitude was a great motivator for J&H'ers, particularly younger ones," Day says.

The Philadelphia office was and is one of J&H's largest. Purnell managed it for eight years, expanding its business and improving its profits, becoming a logical choice to succeed Sexton.

VISION OF OPPORTUNITY IN THE 1970S

Purnell says of his term as chief executive, "If there was any vision, it was the vision of opportunity in the 1970s, because they were boom times, they really were. If you got off your fanny there was plenty of good business to be had, and we had the staff to do it. My thought was just to keep this momentum going and get some discipline in the firm."

He became a voice for the branches. He understood their needs and problems and, in comparison to the period not many years earlier when branch managers ran their businesses without much day-to-day contact with New York, he worked hard to meld the entire J&H network into a cohesive unit focused on the client. During his tenure as CEO, J&H opened offices in regional business centers such as Charlotte, Nashville, Phoenix and Tulsa, extending its branch system beyond the traditional corporate centers such as New York, Philadelphia, Chicago and San Francisco. "New York had a tremendous overhead, and while they serviced a lot of business, they just didn't have the profitability factor you could derive from a branch," he says. "Our future depended on getting a very strong branch system." His strategy was to service more business through the branches and provide support from New York.

To sustain this strategy, he took the then-controversial step of changing the way commissions were shared within the firm. He explains, "When a piece of business was initiated in a branch and they had to get the support of another office, and it was generally the support of the New York office, the commission was split 50-50. Well, there was a feeling in the branches that New York was really not entitled to that, that they were kind of stealing their half of the commission. And you really cannot run a lot of branches on 50 percent of the commission. So after a lot of deliberation, we decided to give the full commission on any piece of business produced by the branch right back to the branch." New York continued to charge for support, but at a much lower rate than 50 percent. This approach benefited the branch as well as the client, since there was no longer a financial disincentive for branch offices to ask New York for help. "It gave us much better teamwork than we had ever had before," he asserts. "That really made an awful lot of difference in the quality of product we gave to the client." This shift in commission split led ultimately to the "single treasury" concept which is central to the way J&H is managed today. Under single treasury, offices do not bill each other for services. For instance, if an employee from Seattle flies to Atlanta to help serve a client there, the Seattle office does not bill the Atlanta office, not even for air fare. Offices are expected to support each other fully, even though they absorb the costs themselves. Cooperation with other J&H offices is a key factor in evaluating a branch manager's performance. The objective is to focus the company's total resources on the client, without letting internal money issues get in the way.

Working with other members of the board, Purnell also changed the firm's compensation structure, introducing employee incentive plans that were predecessors of today's broadly based incentive programs.

Further, many in the firm credit Purnell with bringing greater financial discipline to J&H. Even through Dorrance Sexton's chairmanship, the firm still distributed most of its profits to the directors. "Dick Purnell put a stop to that," Dick Nielsen says. "He insisted on putting money aside to build a war chest to expand the firm. That, in my opinion, is the greatest legacy he left at J&H. Without that, we could not have expanded the way we have and the whole history of J&H would be different."

Purnell also was an outspoken believer in business

Four generations of J&H chief executives posed in the early 1980s. From left, Dick Purnell, CEO from 1972 to 1981; Dorrance Sexton, 1962-72; Elmer Jefferson, 1952-62; and Bob Hatcher, 1981-90.

support of public service institutions. "Business has a lot to offer to the community and has a responsibility to get involved," he maintains. J&H's companywide program of encouraging its people to participate in nonprofit activities of their choice, with financial support from the firm, began during his tenure and has been carried forward by his successors.

Purnell was known as an autocratic and demanding boss who brought needed change to Johnson & Higgins. "He could be tough when he had to be, but there was another side," Gardner Mundy says. "He cared deeply about employees, particularly long-term service people." Director Rufus Williams says, "On a personal level, a wonderful man. But tough. He set very high standards for himself and others. He let you know what was on his mind."

Now retired and living with his wife, Maggie, on Long Island, Purnell looks back proudly to his years at J&H and to the discipline he instilled in the firm. "I never had to cross the street to avoid anybody," he says. "I could look everybody right straight in the eye. When you have integrity and a reputation such as Johnson & Higgins has, it's a wonderful feeling. I can remember chewing out two directors for allowing an employee to stay even one minute after he did something that was inviolate to Johnson & Higgins. I was so mad I almost had a heart attack." Or maybe they did, given just how forceful Purnell could be.

8.

Captives

When I came on the J&H board in 1963," Dick Purnell says, "the word 'captive' could be spoken only behind closed doors. It was anathema. Brokers were so afraid they would lose their position in the conventional market. It was a stop sign for years, and suddenly the attitude changed and the business flooded in."

Retired executive vice president Richard E. Meyer comments, "If there has been a single most dramatic area of growth at Johnson & Higgins over the past 25 years, it is captives. Today, we are far and away the world leader. We did that by anticipating clients' needs."

Captives are insurance companies created to underwrite the risks of their parent corporations. While captives will never dominate the insurance market, they now account for approximately six percent of the property/casualty premiums written each year in the United States and have assumed a permanent place in the panoply of risk financing techniques that are available to corporations.

J&H manages well over 400 captives on behalf of clients, twice as many as its nearest competitor. In Bermuda alone, J&H-managed captives generate approximately $1.3 billion of premium volume each year.

How J&H became the preeminent manager of captive insurance companies is one of the compelling stories in the firm's history. Brian R. Hall has been there from the beginning. Hall is a long-time Bermuda resident who leads the J&H Global Captive Management Group, headquartered on that island colony. In addition to its Bermuda operation, the group has offices in 19 captive domiciles around the world, including Barbados, the Cayman Islands, Dublin, Guernsey, Luxembourg, Singapore and Vermont. Several of its European offices are joint ventures with UNISON partners.

In 1989, Hall was elected to the J&H board of directors, suggesting not only the importance that captives have assumed within the company but also the worldwide scope of J&H today. He became the first non-U.S.-resident director in J&H history — "a trend for the future," he says, "as Johnson & Higgins continues to become more global in its operations."

Origins in Bermuda

Hall relates, "I got into the captive management business in 1963, when it was just starting." An insurance accountant, he joined a firm headed by Fred Reiss, the father of the Bermuda captive movement. At that time, captives were considered to be an exotic idea outside the mainstream of insurance. By 1969, however, Reiss had 14 clients, and corporations and brokers were beginning to take notice. Hall struck out on his own that same year, founding Inter-Ocean Management Limited — with a staff of two employees — just as the captive boom was getting under way. One year later, Inter-Ocean became a subcontractor of captives for J&H for the "princely" fee of $500 a year. "I really thought I'd made it big," Hall recalls with a grin. J&H chose to work initially with Hall, rather than build its own Bermuda operation, to hold down risk in an untested new business.

As it turned out, the alliance of J&H and Inter-Ocean was a marriage made in heaven. Working together, the two firms prospered in captive management. Other brokers, too, began promoting captives, but J&H was more innovative and client-responsive right from the start. Hall believes that J&H established an early lead because of the receptiveness of its account executives, many of whom were quick to recognize how captives could serve the needs of clients. "A very strong advocate right from the beginning was Dick Meyer," he says. "At the time, Dick managed the General Telephone & Electronics account, and GTE was one of the first clients to form a captive."

In fact, the very first joint client of J&H and Inter-Ocean in 1970 was Savannah Company, a property insurance captive of Pennzoil Company. Others, including GTE, followed. It was an exciting time for those in J&H who recognized the potential of captives and got in on the ground floor, helping clients form these insurance subsidiaries.

Meanwhile, Bermuda took an early lead as a captives domicile because of its favorable regulations, tax-free environment and skilled work force — and is still number one today. In the early years, there was a lot of good-natured kidding in the J&H New York office whenever an employee headed off for the lovely resort island on business. "I used to go to Bermuda to have lunch and come back the same day," Dick Rice recalls. "I took a lot of flak, but I'd say, 'Hey, it's like going to Cleveland. What do you think, I'm going to the beach? I go down there to work.'"

On the other hand, Hall notes, "One of the things I was fortunate about in gaining early visibility for the operation is that everybody likes to visit Bermuda."

Why Companies Formed Captives

Why did captives suddenly gain favor? In many cases, they were launched by companies that felt the traditional insurance market wasn't giving them a fair shake. Rice tells the story of an association of savings banks that formed a captive in 1970 to underwrite catastrophe covers on homes on which the banks held mortgages. The banks had previously bought such coverage from commercial carriers, but when premium rates doubled in one year, "the banks went crazy," according to Rice. Working with J&H, they formed a Bermuda captive to control their insurance costs.

Even absent such dire circumstances, there were often solid business reasons for the formation of captives. "Many large companies began to realize that it didn't make sense to insure first dollar coverage with the commercial insurance companies when there was a predictability of loss in the primary areas of exposure," Hall says. "In fact, the market was imposing higher and higher deductibles, so companies began to use captives to

The Johnson & Higgins Global Captive Management Group is headquartered in Victoria Hall in Hamilton, Bermuda. Below, the view from the office roof.

CAPTIVES

formalize the self-insurance of that risk."

Moreover, as corporations expanded globally, they were unable to purchase property insurance on a uniform basis worldwide. While substantial deductibles were available in the United States, plants overseas were often forced by local rules to purchase property insurance from the first dollar — an irksome and unnecessary cost, from the viewpoint of many risk managers. One solution was to purchase full-coverage policies and have the underwriters of these policies reinsure the first $50,000 or $100,000 with a captive owned by the American parent.

As more companies established captives, their use became a hot topic among risk managers. "The risk managers would mingle at RIMS and other conferences, and one manager would say, 'I have a captive, do you?'," Hall relates. "That's how it really evolved. The clients would go to their account executives at J&H and say, 'What's this I hear about captives? Tell me more.' So there was a scramble within J&H at the client relationship level to be fully informed and get on board."

Companies were also attracted by the tax breaks, including the deductibility of premiums paid to a captive. In 1977, however, the Internal Revenue Service slammed the door shut, stating in ruling 77-316 that premiums paid to a captive were not deductible. "Some brokers whistled and cheered because they thought captives were dead," Meyer says. "Well, we had never suggested to a client that they set up a captive for tax purposes, so none of our clients had any anticipation of a tax deduction. When 77-316 came out, it was a neutral event as far as we were concerned."

THE ACQUISITION OF INTER-OCEAN

By 1979, Inter-Ocean was managing over 100 Bermuda captives, primarily through its agreement with J&H. At that point, seeking to solidify its position, J&H offered to acquire Inter-Ocean. Hall says, "They thought, 'How long-term is Brian Hall? What happens if he goes under a bus?'" Hall says he was "very apprehensive" about giv-

Johnson & Higgins Intermediaries

The Global Captive Management Group is only one part of J&H's growing operations in Bermuda. Also situated on the island is Johnson & Higgins Intermediaries, which provides J&H retail offices, UNISON partners and other brokers with access to the Bermuda underwriting market.

Since 1985, nearly $10 billion has been invested in new underwriting capacity in Bermuda, mainly for catastrophe reinsurance and excess liability coverage. "The Bermuda scene today is clearly one of the focal points for buyers of insurance worldwide," says L. John Goldberg, senior vice president in charge of Johnson & Higgins Intermediaries. "This market can be accessed only through a local broker. We provide that service, meeting the needs of J&H corporate clients and the insurance firms. We also place some reinsurance for captive companies."

Dick Nielsen remarks, "Bermuda is growing faster than any other insurance market in the world, and going forward it has every sign of continuing to grow significantly both on a retail and a reinsurance basis. I think it will be a much bigger part of our life than in the past."

J&H began advertising its captives management skills in the 1970s, when the use of captives was rapidly gaining popularity in corporate America.

How will a captive perform for you? J&H can give you a preview now.

In one way or another, your company is probably retaining larger and larger portions of its liability exposures.

However, choosing the optimal funding arrangement for such risk assumption requires extremely careful risk management analysis.

Consider, for example, the complexities of the captive approach alone. What risks should it accept? Should it be set up off-shore? What about the IRS? Is adequate reinsurance available?

Ignoring any of the variables can cause big problems. For instance, a group of teaching hospitals recently found that its proposed captive could not arrange needed excess coverage from reinsurers. Johnson & Higgins was then invited to study the problem and spotted the organizational flaw. The coverage was soon obtained.

If you want the best possible help in forming a captive, call J&H. Our advanced risk management techniques include exclusive software programs that instantaneously preview your working captive. There is no need to guess about choosing the funding alternative that makes the most sense for you. The nearest J&H office can give you full details.

Johnson & Higgins

The private insurance broker.
We answer only to you.

A group of J&H risk management specialists in captive funding:
Richard J. Rice, New York; Patrick J.T. Stephenson, Bermuda;
Roger Thomas, Los Angeles; and George H. Shattuck, Jr., Boston.

RISK AND INSURANCE MANAGEMENT SERVICES; EMPLOYEE BENEFIT AND ACTUARIAL CONSULTING. THROUGHOUT THE WORLD

ing up his independence and thought long and hard about what to do. Finally, his friend Gardner Mundy, then general counsel of J&H (and now general counsel and a director), told him that J&H would not interfere with his operation as long as it remained successful. So Hall sold the company to J&H and continued as president. He adds, "And then the finance manuals arrived, the procedures manuals arrived. All of a sudden I realized I was employed rather than self-employed. But we got through that and, in fact, Gardner's prediction proved to be right."

Captives surged to new heights of popularity in the mid-1980s, when an exceptionally hard insurance market forced corporations to look for new risk-financing solutions. And then something unexpected happened. Even when the insurance market returned to relative normalcy, the use of captives continued to grow. "Basically, once rates went back down it became clear that the world had changed," says J&H vice president Robert G. Petrie III. "Companies were going to insure a whole lot less and were going to assume a lot more risk." Assuming more risk translates, of course, into the increased use of captives and other self-insurance techniques.

Today, captives are a way of life in corporate America, and J&H continues to expand in this important business. It is helping clients form over 50 new captives a year. David Olsen points out, "Our job as a broker, as a problem-solver, is to say, 'If the traditional marketplace doesn't meet your needs, we'll solve them in another way.' And one of those ways is captives."

One of the newest twists is the growing use of captives to enhance a parent company's profits, not just solve its risk management problems. "We are getting into the central business issues of companies," says Roger Gillett, senior vice president in the Global Captive Management Group. For instance, some companies, such as computer and auto manufacturers, now sell or give away insurance products from a captive to support the sale of products. Others, such as banks, use captives to write credit life insurance policies for outstanding loan or credit card balances.

In addition, the captive movement, once primarily a U.S. phenomenon, is spreading globally. Indeed, one of the Global Captive Management Group's main strategies is to work with J&H offices and UNISON partners around the world to help non-U.S. companies form captives. Currently, about 80 percent of the group's clients are U.S.-based, but that percentage is expected to decline as the use of captives by non-U.S. corporations accelerates. The group is targeting growth in Europe, the Far East and Latin America. In Mexico, for instance, the group is working with UNISON partner Brockman y Schuh to develop captives for existing clients and attract new clients. Similar programs are under way in other countries.

Team Effort

Years ago, most brokers viewed captives as a competitive threat. Rod Day notes, "Traditionalists said, 'Oh my gosh, all that primary insurance commission is going to disappear and go to those captive companies.'" But for J&H, at least, exactly the opposite has occurred. "We didn't lose any income," Meyer reports. "We enhanced our income because we were still able to get commissions to service the business in the United States, we got a captive management fee and in some cases we got a reinsurance intermediary commission."

Speaking of J&H's position in captive management today, Gillett concludes, "J&H has the dominant position, certainly. Within the J&H system, we've just about beaten that point to death. I'm almost embarrassed to go out there one more time and say, 'Did you know we're twice as big as any of our competitors?' When I make presentations to the branches, I try to make very clear that the Global Captive Management Group has been a great success story and it's a result of the work of a team. And part of the team is them — the 'them' being the branch system and the UNISON partners. We can help with specific projects for their clients, but they're the ones who make it happen on a day-to-day basis. We wouldn't be what we are today without the J&H branches and the UNISON system."

9.

Bob Hatcher: The Kitchen Table Approach

In 1977, Dick Purnell visited the J&H branch in Richmond, ostensibly because he had never been there before. The office was headed by Robert V. Hatcher, Jr., 47, an astute Virginian who had been elected to the J&H board two years earlier. "Dick came into the office and met everybody and made a little speech," Hatcher recalls. "Then we took him out to the just-finished Philip Morris cigarette manufacturing plant, which was state of the art. Dick was just restless. He wasn't interested at all."

Hatcher had arranged for Purnell to join a group of friends for dinner, but Purnell insisted on returning first to his motel to change his shirt. Hatcher continues, "I said, 'No, you don't have to do that,' but he said, 'Damn it, I do and you're coming with me.'" At the motel, after Purnell had changed, Hatcher asked whether he was ready. Hatcher continues, "He said, 'No, I'm not ready. Are you ready?' And I said, 'Yes, I'm ready.' He said, 'Are you ready to be president of Johnson & Higgins?' I was totally nonplussed." That is how Bob Hatcher learned he would become the next J&H president.

Hatcher wasn't entirely sure he wanted the job. "I decided if, for whatever reason, I wouldn't take the presidency, I would resign from the firm," he says. "At least five or six other directors had agreed with Dick on the selection. I didn't think it would be right to turn them down and stay comfortably in Richmond." After talking it over with his wife, who looked forward to moving to

Dick Purnell, left, brought Bob Hatcher to New York as his heir-apparent in 1977. Four years later, Hatcher succeeded Purnell as chief executive.

Reinsurance

Once a skeleton in Johnson & Higgins' closet, Willcox Incorporated Reinsurance Intermediaries has blossomed into a vital, vibrant part of the company. Willcox is one of two reinsurance brokers owned by J&H. The other is a Lloyd's of London broker, Willcox Johnson & Higgins Ltd., part of Johnson & Higgins Ltd. It was formerly Carter Brito e Cunha Ltd. and was acquired in 1987.

J&H was one of the pioneers in reinsurance brokerage, entering the field in 1923 when it acquired Albert Willcox & Company, the nation's oldest reinsurance intermediary. Despite this early lead, W.H. LaBoyteaux, who headed J&H from 1916 to 1947, was not interested in reinsurance and let Willcox's business languish. Speaking of LaBoyteaux's attitude, one retired director comments, "He said something to the effect that taking care of direct customers is a full-time job and he did not intend to get involved in any extraneous businesses."

After World War II, as property values rose and liability awards soared, insurance companies increased the use of reinsurance to reduce their exposures, and J&H soon recognized it was missing out on a golden opportunity. However, repeated attempts to revitalize Willcox failed. By the early 1980s, J&H management considered closing or selling the subsidiary, but finally decided to make one last attempt to turn it around. In 1984, in a dramatic move, Willcox was restructured as a joint venture with Willis Faber, which acquired a 49 percent interest in the company. As part of the reorganization, Willcox withdrew from the broking of facultative reinsurance in order to concentrate on treaty reinsurance, a more profitable segment. In addition, Johnson & Higgins put one of its top executives — Ken Hecken, a respected member of the J&H board — in charge of Willcox. "At that time Willcox had about 12 branch offices and about 350 people and was losing $1 million a year," Hecken recalls. "So we restaffed the company completely. Two years later we were down to 120 people, and only ten of those were part of the original 350. And we were down to one office." Today, Willcox has a staff of 220 located in four offices in the United States, as well as in London and Singapore.

The joint venture arrangement with Willis Faber lasted only five years. At the end of 1988, J&H bought back Willis Faber's stake because of disagreements over how Willcox should be run. Nonetheless, the reorganization worked. "When you take a company like this, break it down into its pieces, clean off the parts, throw most of them away, and rebuild it from scratch, guess what you get?" says Willis T. King, Jr., who succeeded Hecken as CEO in 1985 and chairman in 1986. "You get a company that's made from an iron core with a tough group of people who have been to hell and back with a good common philosophy."

Willcox made a modest profit in 1984 and has steadily increased its earnings ever since. Moreover, versus a market share of less than one percent prior to the reorganization, Willcox now holds nearly 10 percent of the U.S. reinsurance brokerage market. "We continue to grow rapidly and have become a significant contributor to J&H profits," King points out.

Willcox serves a range of clients. It has shares of the reinsurance placements of most of the large stockholder-owned insurance companies; serves many smaller mutual companies in farm regions across the United States; and is the number one marine reinsurance broker in the U.S. In addition, a large component of Willcox's revenue derives from non-U.S. business, which principally involves ceding companies in Europe and Japan and some in the Middle East.

Reinsurance brokerage, in King's view, is an oligopoly dominated by a few large firms, offering excellent opportunities for a smaller firm like Willcox to develop strong niche positions. "The way we look at it," he says, "until we get above a 20 percent market share we're not going to threaten anyone enough so that they worry about us and try to slow us down."

Bob Hatcher is a native Virginian who grew up in a southern tradition of horses, hunting and the outdoors.

New York, he accepted the promotion.

Purnell continued as chairman and CEO, grooming Hatcher to be his successor, just as Dorrance Sexton had groomed him. Four years later, near the end of 1981, Purnell stepped down and Hatcher became CEO, serving until his own retirement at the end of 1990. Hatcher's nine-year tenure as chairman was marked by continued growth, but also by some very difficult conditions in the insurance market with intense pressure on brokers' profit margins. "He led the firm through some challenging times," Dick Rice remarks.

A True Southern Gentleman

With his soft drawl, gracious manner and ever-present humor, Hatcher is a sophisticated southern gentleman. Dick Nielsen points out, "Bob Hatcher can be the most charming man alive. He's a fun guy and people enjoy being with him." As chairman, Hatcher emphasized the importance of developing personal relationships in business and espoused "the kitchen table approach." One former J&H staff member says, "He believed you could get more done at the kitchen table at two in the morning

Under Hatcher's leadership, J&H moved into handsome new offices at 125 Broad Street in lower Manhattan. Here, he poses on the senior executive floor of the new facilities.

over a glass of wine than you could at a formal meeting in the office." This philosophy played especially well with J&H's European UNISON partners, who felt at home with Hatcher and appreciated his style of mixing business and pleasure. Hatcher traveled often to Europe to spend time with the principals of J&H's correspondents, dining with them, hunting with them, even attending their children's weddings.

Hatcher is known, as well, for his active involvement in worthy causes. He served as chairman of the board of The College of Insurance, guiding it through a critical period following the construction of its building in lower Manhattan. He served also on the boards of the University of Virginia, the Virginia Museum of Fine Arts, The Seeing Eye and many other organizations. Even today, he is involved with half a dozen nonprofit institutions, including a board seat on the Thomas Jefferson Memorial Foundation, which owns Monticello.

Explaining his belief that business people should participate in public service, he says, "Somebody has to do it, so it might as well be the somebodys who have some influence and an organization on which they can depend."

Hatcher was born in Richmond, where his father was a prominent attorney and later president of Atlantic Life Insurance Company. Young Bob attended Hampden-Sydney College in Hampden-Sydney, Virginia, for three years. However, when he failed third-year Latin by one point, his father "went into a tailspin" and became so angry at the Latin professor that he insisted Bob transfer to the University of Virginia, from which Bob received a bachelor's degree in economics in 1953. (Massie Valentine, a J&H director and Richmond native who has known Bob since they were teenagers, says, "Mr. Hatcher was always very hard driving and outspoken. Bob inherited a lot of that. He has all this energy and is full of ideas and can be very demanding.") On graduation, Hatcher

No More Booze, Ho Hum

One of the all-time J&H tempests in a teapot occurred in May 1982, when the company issued a memo asking its New York employees not to drink at lunch. The missive was leaked to the press, whereupon wags had a field day. Twitting J&H for being "staid and sober," the *Wall Street Journal* said the memo was drawing "guffaws from rival brokers." A TV crew camped out in the J&H lobby to ask employees whether their rights were being violated — and then broadcast a playful account on the evening news. There was also widespread bemusement within the company itself. One jokester penned a parody, "The Ballad of Water and Wall" (the title refers to the location of J&H's office at the time), which was circulated surreptitiously throughout the New York headquarters. Two sample stanzas:

There are strange things done, 'neath the mid-day sun
At the corner of Water and Wall
And that cynical joker, the Oldest Broker,
Who's cursed with total recall,
Says that May the eleventh of Eighty-Two
Was the day that was darkest of all.
He remembers them well: the mournful knell
That Black Friday tolled o'er the Street.
December the seventh of 'forty-one, when we lost our Pacific fleet.
But the worst day yet, he's prepared to bet,
(And one can't see how he can lose)
Was the tragic day, in the month of May,
When J&H banned the booze.

Today, the whole subject seems like ancient history. Lots of companies now ask employees not to drink at lunch. And in any event, the memo was never strictly enforced. Rather than being rigid company policy, alcohol-free lunches have evolved into being part of J&H's culture. The topic barely causes a stir with anybody any more.

served in the Counterintelligence Corps with the U.S. Army in Korea before returning to Richmond and starting his career with a small local insurance agency.

In 1959, Hatcher joined the Baker-Cockrell Agency in that city, soon becoming a partner. "Bob was definitely on his way up," Valentine says. "He was clearly one of the top two or three young people in the brokerage business in Richmond. Bob meets people easily and they like him. He's also very smart. He was working for a good firm and was doing well."

Baker-Cockrell had several major, prestigious clients, including A.H. Robins Company. However, Tom Cockrell was getting along in years and his daughter had been in a terrible automobile accident and would require medical care the rest of her life. Cockrell therefore decided to sell the agency to raise cash for his daughter's care, and he asked a friend at Aetna Casualty & Surety Company to put out feelers to Johnson & Higgins. J&H already had several clients in Virginia, serviced primarily out of Philadelphia and New York, and welcomed the chance to expand its local presence. "Dorrance Sexton called initially," Hatcher recollects. "I talked with him over the phone and was very impressed. Then he sent us some figures, and six weeks went by and Dick Henshaw came down." Other national brokers were seeking to buy the agency and, in fact, one offered a higher price. Nonetheless, Cockrell and Hatcher chose J&H because they felt confident about its plans in Richmond and were comfortable with its senior executives.

Baker-Cockrell, renamed Johnson & Higgins of Virginia, Inc., with Hatcher as its president, didn't waste any time getting integrated into J&H. "We were legally Johnson & Higgins of Virginia on a certain day, and Dorrance Sexton called to congratulate us," Hatcher says. "Joan Charles answered the phone, 'Johnson & Higgins.' That was the right way to do it and it impressed Dorrance. He didn't expect to hear that."

Under Hatcher's leadership, the Richmond office flourished. Drawing on the resources of J&H, it was able to offer new services, such as international and loss reserve analysis, and it expanded geographically into North Carolina, West Virginia and other markets. When the office was acquired by J&H, it had just seven employees. Seven years later in 1975, when Hatcher was elected to the Johnson & Higgins board of directors, it had nearly 100.

DEVELOPMENT OF STRATEGIC PLANNING

In 1977, when he moved to New York to assume the J&H presidency, Hatcher concentrated initially on domestic operations. He emphasized marketing and demonstrated a commitment to change — for instance, setting in motion a series of studies that led to the creation of an energy resource task force to seek major oil company accounts, a previous J&H weakness.

And then came an important shift in J&H's direction. Shortly before Purnell retired as CEO, he read *Top Management Strategy* by Benjamin B. Tregoe and John W. Zimmerman. "This was unusual for Dick because he normally didn't do that kind of reading," Hatcher says. "He did it really, I guess, for me and for the firm. After he read the book, he gave it to me and said, 'I want you to read this and then I want you to act on it. We have never had any strategic planning in this firm, so get going.' And we did."

Soon thereafter, Hatcher held a series of strategic planning meetings at a retreat in Westchester County, just north of New York City. These meetings, which have become an annual event, set the tone for his tenure as CEO. "We learned a lot about ourselves," he says. "It was like looking in the mirror." From those early meetings came a detailed strategic plan with nearly 30 objectives, including stepped-up international growth, increased emphasis on consulting services, a more systematic approach to serving mid-sized accounts, the restructuring of senior management responsibilities and a stronger marketing effort. Gardner Mundy views this period as a time of "gradual and grudging recognition that J&H was now a large company."

These events occurred within the context of a tumultuous environment in the insurance market. Early in the decade of the '80s, a soft market cut into premiums and commissions. Later in the decade, an unusually hard market prompted many corporations to self-insure more risks and rely less on the conventional insurance market. Even after the hard market abated, corporations continued to use the conventional market less and employ alternative risk financing techniques more.

J&H responded to the hardening of the market and its aftermath in two main ways. First, the company expanded its risk management consulting services and beefed up its capabilities in alternative market programs. In addition, insurance brokers were under attack as messengers of the bad news that businesses could no longer obtain certain types of insurance coverage, such as directors and officers liability — or, if they could, would have to pay dearly for it. Uniquely among brokers, J&H launched a nationwide advertising campaign that discussed the liability crisis, tort reform, insurance costs and the role of brokers. The ad program was part of a general strengthening of J&H's communications activities, internal and external.

Hatcher also broke with tradition and moved the company into upscale offices at 125 Broad Street at the southern tip of Manhattan. The move occurred in 1986. "No more shabby gentility," was his comment at the time. J&H had for years maintained an austere facade, fearful that clients would object if its quarters seemed too elegant. But Hatcher took a different view. "We made the decision," he says, "to spend some money and look like what we are: a leader in international broking and consulting."

GLOBAL GROWTH

Hatcher's greatest love was the firm's international operations, to which he devoted much of his energy as chairman. Although he did not have any international experience when he became president, "by the time he retired, he had become very international in his perspective," Christian Dahms of UNISON partner Jauch & Hübener observes.

J&H had been the first major U.S. broker to establish

Left, in 1970 J&H moved to 95 Wall Street, initially occupying eight floors. By the mid-1980s, it was running out of space and sought new quarters. Right, 125 Broad Street under construction at the southern tip of Manhattan. (125 Broad is the shorter of the two buildings.) Seth Faison took the photo from his apartment in Brooklyn Heights.

an overseas presence in the 1950s, and by the early 1980s it was still doing well. However, Hatcher saw a need to become more aggressive in the face of increased competition. Of special significance was the formation of UNISON at the beginning of the Hatcher years.

His policy was to seek to acquire equity interests in J&H's key correspondents only when the principals of those firms wanted to sell. He believes other U.S. brokers lost opportunities to acquire top overseas firms by making premature bids. "Almost all the firms we were linked to were family-owned," he says. "You just don't push these people around. All we asked was an opportunity to invest when they were ready, and now it's paying dividends."

In 1989, for instance, J&H purchased a 25 percent equity interest in Gil y Carvajal, S.A., a UNISON partner and the premier broker in Spain. The acquisition came about when Hatcher received a phone call late one night from the firm's head, Santiago Gil de Biedma, saying he was prepared to sell an interest to J&H. "He never would have called in the middle of the night if we hadn't been good friends, and he never would have sold us a piece of the firm if he didn't believe in us," Hatcher says. Today, J&H owns 50 percent of Gil y Carvajal.

THE OWNERSHIP ISSUE

Hatcher's greatest disappointment was his inability to convince his partners that J&H should seek an infusion of capital from outside investors. He strove long and

J&H's headquarters building at 125 Broad is a sleek 40-story office tower. J&H and co-tenant Sullivan & Cromwell each bought an equity interest in the structure in early 1995.

hard to arrange a merger with J&H's long-time British correspondent, Willis Faber, but was never able to get the J&H board to go along (see Chapter 10). In addition, he argued that J&H should go public or seek an outside partner, again to no avail.

"It's been my contention for a long time," he says, "and I've expressed it to the board, that part of this firm should be sold. The model is Morgan Stanley. Do exactly what they did. [In 1986, Morgan Stanley made a public offering of 20 percent of its stock.] Or Goldman Sachs. They sold part of their firm to Japanese investors."

There was considerable debate over what course J&H should take, and ultimately Hatcher's view was rejected. David Olsen is among those who believe J&H's structure of private ownership continues to serve the firm and its clients and employees well. He says, "For J&H today, the advantages of being privately owned outweigh the advantages of public ownership or merging or selling a large stake to an outside investor. But we do look at this issue periodically because we may need to raise capital some day. Accepting outside investment would be one way to do that. There are other ways also, however, and we would prefer to meet our capital requirements while remaining a private company. Our decisions on this matter will continue to be based on what is best for clients and staff."

Ed Knetzger Becomes President

Edwin L. Knetzger, Jr., played an important role in the early years of the Hatcher administration, serving as president from 1982 until he retired in 1985. Knetzger is older than Hatcher, so there was never any thought he would become chairman. He remembers his years in the presidency as being "fabulous, unbelievable, ridiculous, maddening, sensational, terrific."

Knetzger is one of the exceptionally upbeat personalities in the history of Johnson & Higgins. He joined the company in 1959 in the New York Employee Benefits Department and later managed the Philadelphia office, which became a feeder of talented employees to the branch system. He believes strongly that a branch manager has a responsibility to develop young people and give them the opportunity to advance and move out to other offices. Many individuals who have risen to high positions in the company were hired or mentored by Knetzger.

Knetzger is very people-oriented. After he returned to New York and became president, he loved to roam the halls and drop in on employees to ask about their work. A J&H vice president says, "He would drop by unannounced. No pretense. He would turn a chair around and sit in it, leaning over the back. That was the Knetzger trademark."

"Something Which Is Quite First Class"

After Hatcher retired, he and his wife, Martha Anne, returned to Virginia, where they now live. He remains active in the community and sits on the boards of several companies and organizations.

Hatcher's eyes light up when he recalls his years at J&H and his career in insurance brokerage. "It's a fascinating business," he says. "You learn a little bit about everything. You can specialize. You can become a super-specialist. If you want, you can deal with nothing but aviation insurance. Or you can learn just enough about aviation insurance and about other types of insurance to call on a prospect. No day is the same as the one before it or the one after it. You're dealing with an investment banking account one afternoon and the next morning there's a workers comp problem at a metals company. And then there's a cargo opportunity down in the Norfolk area, and you're just going like blazes."

In his wallet, Hatcher carries a dog-eared card which reads: "Former Prime Minister Harold Macmillan on his service in the Queen's Life Guards. 'It is a great thing at some time in your life to be associated with something which is quite first class.'" He looks at the card and says, "I think we're lucky, any of us who have had that opportunity."

10.

The Ninety-Eight-Year Handshake

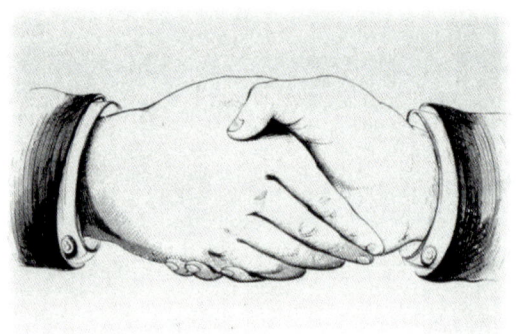

Although executives sometimes gripe about attorneys, there is not a single major company on earth today that would enter an international business deal without legal counsel. It would simply be unthinkable. On the other hand, consider the case of Johnson & Higgins and Willis, Faber & Co. They started doing business with each other in 1892. Seven years later, they became exclusive correspondents — that is, J&H agreed to use Willis as its only broker when placing marine insurance in England and Willis agreed to place marine insurance in the United States solely through J&H. For the next several years, the two firms tried to put their agreement of exclusivity into writing. They discussed, haggled and negotiated, but could never quite get the terms down on paper the way they wanted.

In 1977, Willis Faber moved to an historic London building at Ten Trinity Square. Erected early in the century for the Port of London Authority, the structure's emblems and statues have a theme of navigation and commerce.

Finally, on July 16, 1903, David Willis of Willis Faber wrote in frustration to James B. Dickson, president of J&H, proclaiming, "To frame a legal document to the satisfaction of the lawyers seems such an interminable business that personally I feel inclined to revert to your idea of having a mere informal understanding that we divide our joint profits from every source in the proportions agreed upon." One advantage of an unwritten agreement, he pointed out, was that either party could simply withdraw from the relationship if dissatisfied.

One month later, Dickson replied, "We long since became disgusted with the technicalities which the legal fraternity are so insistent upon including in documents of this character.... It would seem to me as if an informal understanding would answer every purpose."

And that was that. Thereafter, these two major brokerage companies worked together without ever signing a formal agreement. Either firm could have gone its separate way at a moment's notice. Yet, for nearly a century, they maintained their transatlantic alliance without a written contract. For that reason, it was surely one of the most remarkable relationships in business history and was described as follows in a J&H publication: "Based on equal measures of mutual respect and enlightened self-interest, the friendly, highly flexible arrangement encourages each organization to keep its separate identity while drawing, as appropriate, on the other's special strengths."

The relationship was a boon to both parties. Over time, the firms expanded their agreement to cover other categories of insurance in addition to marine. By the late 1980s, J&H and its UNISON partners were providing

Lloyd's of London is one of the world's great institutions. Founded in the seventeenth century in the coffeehouse of Edward Lloyd, it was originally organized to underwrite marine insurance but now issues almost any kind of coverage.

several hundred million dollars of premium income to Willis each year on insurance placed in the British market. What is more, J&H and Willis established joint ventures around the world — for insurance brokerage in Australia, New Zealand and Canada and for reinsurance and surplus lines brokerage in the United States, although these ventures were governed by written contracts. J&H even bought a five percent equity interest in Willis to help cement the relationship. One industry publication mused that J&H and Willis "have been holding each other's hands since, it seems, they both stepped down from the Ark."

This long-standing business affiliation — and how it came apart in 1990 — stands as a unique chapter in Johnson & Higgins history. Looking back today, Don Carlson, manager of the J&H St. Louis office, says, "We had a long relationship and it was a good one. That's what should be emphasized, not the rancor of the final few months. We did a lot with them, and our clients benefited."

Or, as Dick Meyer observes kiddingly, "As I said to our people, it was 98 years and we found out it just didn't work. So we went on to something else."

J&H has been a Lloyd's of London broker since 1987 through the acquisition of Carter Brito e Cunha Ltd., now Johnson & Higgins Ltd.

Shipowners Claims Bureau

Even as Johnson & Higgins celebrates its 150th anniversary in 1995, it looks forward in 1997 to the 70th birthday of one of its oldest and most unusual subsidiaries, Shipowners Claims Bureau, Inc. John H. Cassedy, now retired as SCB's chief executive, likes to call SCB "the jewel in Johnson & Higgins' crown."

SCB manages the American Steamship Owners Mutual Protection & Indemnity Association, a nonprofit mutual insurance company better known as The American Club. Most shipowners carry two basic insurances: hull coverage, placed in the London market and other underwriting centers, and protection and indemnity, insured primarily through P&I mutual clubs around the world. "Prior to World War I, most P&I coverage was placed with the London clubs," says Thomas J. McGowan, chief executive officer of SCB. "However, due to the exigencies of the war, in 1917 J&H founded the first and only American club." J&H managed the club directly until 1927, when it established SCB as an independent subsidiary to take on that assignment.

The club's members include most of the major U.S. shipowners. In its managerial role, SCB performs the rating and underwriting for the club, collects premiums, adjusts losses, reimburses the owner-members and invests the club's portfolio. In addition to managing The American Club, SCB handles claims and average adjusting work in the United States for overseas P&I clubs. One of its most famous assignments was to settle claims arising from the sinking of the *Andrea Doria* in 1956.

"We're in a fascinating business that helps carry forward the tradition of J&H leadership in marine insurance," McGowan states.

When the *Andrea Doria* sank off Nantucket in 1956, Shipowners Claims Bureau represented the underwriters in settling insurance claims.

How It All Began

The relationship was born of necessity. In the late nineteenth century, marine-insurance broking was the heart and soul of Johnson & Higgins. On the other hand, after the U.S. Civil War marine hull underwriting capacity gravitated to London, particularly to Lloyd's. J&H needed access to this capacity for its clients. And since it did not have a London office, it arranged to place insurance through British brokers, a common industry practice then as now.

J&H worked originally with two brokers, John D. Tyson of Liverpool and a Mr. Tyler of London. Then along came Stephen Loines. Loines was a prominent New York broker who had been in business with one Charles A. Wreaks. When Wreaks died in 1892, Loines joined J&H as a partner, one of only five at the time. His influence within this small group was felt immediately.

Wreaks & Loines had used Henry Willis & Co. (as Willis Faber was then called) as its British correspondent, and Loines recommended the London firm to his new partners at J&H. And so it was that in June 1892 Loines and another J&H partner, John Barrett, set sail from New York on the *St. Paul* for Southampton, England, to establish a correspondent relationship with Willis. They were successful in making these arrangements, and for the next seven years J&H placed insurance in the British market through Willis while also continuing to use Tyler and Tyson.

The relationship went smoothly for a time. As the 1890s drew to a close, however, Willis began to grumble about the financial terms of the pact, under which Willis received 45 percent of the commissions and J&H retained 55 percent. One of the Willis partners, Edwin J. Spencer, summarized his firm's complaint in a memoir written years later: "The result of our success with the International fleet was that we got more of Johnson & Higgins' business; but... the scale of commission which we accepted from them in the beginning was made intentionally bare. It was admittedly temporary, but when, however, we tried to readjust it, we found that we could not get into agreement with them."

Back and forth across the Atlantic went letter after letter, with Willis asking for a larger share of the commissions and J&H requesting "a little more patience," insisting that the economics of the business being placed in London did not immediately justify paying a larger portion to Willis. In 1899, in an effort to resolve the growing conflict, Loines and Barrett set sail again for England on the *St. Paul*, arriving on a Wednesday for a brief visit. What happened during their four days in Southampton is one of the more unusual episodes in J&H history. Spencer of the Willis firm described the events as follows:

> In the time thus at our disposal we talked day and night in our sitting-room at the Southampton hotel, and the result was that upon the Friday night, finding agreement impossible, we definitely settled to break off business relations between our two firms; but such a sentimental atmosphere had been engendered that we protested mutual, everlasting friendship notwithstanding....
>
> When, however, we met at breakfast on the Saturday morning, Barrett, after an avalanche of jokes, most unexpectedly agreed to accept our terms; but we continued talking from the breakfast table to his cabin on board the steamer, and then backwards and forwards on the gangway, until he was pushed back to the deck of the steamer and I on the quay, and we shouted to each other in the distance as the steamer got under way.

There were, of course, good business reasons to continue the relationship, which had become important to both firms. The affiliation gave J&H access to the London market through a premier English firm. And it brought Willis large amounts of business from the number one marine broker in America.

Out of the 1899 negotiations in Southampton emerged a plan for J&H and Willis to expand their relationship, not abandon it. J&H would access the British market exclusively through Willis, and Willis would no longer accept marine business for any other U.S. broker. Moreover, J&H agreed to split commissions 50-50, just as Willis had proposed. Willis, for its part, agreed to compensate Tyler and Tyson for having supplanted them as J&H correspondents; this point was included at the insistence of J&H, which felt an obligation to its old friends in Liverpool and London. At last, David Willis wrote several months later, "we are all quite content."

Although this agreement would undergo some modifications in the years that followed, it established the basic principles of the J&H-Willis affiliation, and these principles would remain unchanged.

A quarter century later, in 1924, J&H President W.H. LaBoyteaux sought to put these principles — until then discussed in conversations and letters, but never written down definitively — onto a single sheet of paper for the first time. He drafted a memo, which he called "the idea of the agreement as it was intended." His memo contained four simple points:

1. The arrangement was exclusive.
2. Either party was free to cancel it at any time.
3. Neither party was to depart from the agreement without consulting the other.
4. Neither party was to circumvent the agreement to secure new business or a new market.

This fourth point was actually a new twist on the original pact and sprang directly from J&H's 1924 acquisition of Willcox, Peck & Hughes, a leading insurance broker based in Cleveland. Willcox had used another firm, not Willis, as its English correspondent. When J&H suggested it was free to continue placing Willcox business through that other firm, Willis Faber protested. In effect, the fourth point acknowledged the need to discuss such matters in advance.

How the Relationship Flourished

From those simple, turn-of-the-century beginnings, the volume of business between J&H and Willis grew steadily over the years. Moreover, the relationship evolved into something far more than just a business alliance. Many long-time J&Hers still speak fondly of the warm personal friendships they established with the people of Willis Faber. David Winton, who spent 44 years at J&H before retiring in 1979, recalls his first visit to London in 1943. He was on leave from J&H for wartime duty in the Office of Strategic Services and, on arriving in London, decided to phone Len Southall of Willis. Winton and Southall had communicated frequently by cable prior to the war, but had never met in person. In his 1987 book, *Recollections of Johnson & Higgins, 1935-1979*, Winton says that on phoning Southall, "He welcomed me more warmly than I could have imagined, and immediately asked me to come down 'to the City' the very next morning." On arriving at the Willis office, Winton was given a grand tour and spent the better part of the day with Southall. The two became "fast friends," visiting often after the war, and maintained that friendship even after both had retired.

The special nature of the J&H-Willis Faber alliance was further demonstrated by the many gifts the two firms exchanged over the years. In 1968, for instance, Willis presented J&H with a scale model of a clipper ship, symbolic of the firms' mutual origins in the broking of marine insurance. And in 1977, J&H gave Willis a grandfather clock bearing the inscription: "This clock was presented by Johnson & Higgins to Willis Faber Limited on the occasion of their move to Ten Trinity Square and in recognition and appreciation of a friendship and valued relationship that knows no bounds in time."

In his 1987 book, Winton remarked, "It may well be the longest and most successful 'partnership' of wholly separate firms, each marching to a different corporate drum, but marching together toward joint and common goals."

How the Relationship Ended

However, even as Winton wrote those words, the alliance was fraying at the edges. L. John Goldberg, for one, thought the sense of trust was breaking down. Assigned to London in 1985 as J&H's liaison to Willis, he found there was "a great relationship between Bob

Hatcher and David Palmer," then chairmen of their respective firms, but he came to believe that this relationship did not carry down as fully as it should to employees at the day-to-day working level.

Both sides recognized they had a problem, and in 1986 they held a high-level conference, London Bridge I, in New York to discuss mutual concerns. Out of that conference came a Declaration of Unity, circulated to employees of both firms and pledging to move forward in a spirit of partnership. The following year, continuing their dialogue, London Bridge II was held in England.

The firms also began to negotiate a possible merger. Merger talks had been held sporadically for at least a quarter century and were conducted almost non-stop beginning in 1985. Dick Purnell, J&H chief executive from 1972 to 1981, says, "The thing that happened in my time is that Willis always wanted to have an exchange of shares. They wanted to get into the American market — desperately." Purnell opposed a merger, although his successor, Bob Hatcher, favored one, feeling it would benefit both firms. However, Hatcher was never able to convince a majority of the J&H board to go along. In turn, Hatcher's successor, David Olsen, was against the idea of merging. "I was more of a proponent of 'we can do without them' when we were discussing some way to join together," Olsen states. "They had more to lose by not getting together. In other words, we were bringing far more business to the table. But they weren't willing to recognize that or pay for it."

One J&H executive estimates that Willis derived approximately 10 percent of its revenue from U.S. business placed by J&H. Willis executives repeatedly expressed a desire to increase their firm's participation in the U.S. market, and one obvious way would have been to merge with J&H. Peter Bickett, who retired as a J&H director in 1985, says, "There were endless meetings. Johnson & Higgins directors would go over to London and senior executives of Willis would come here, but we could never come to terms with each other's needs and demands."

Merger negotiations failed for reasons other than price. Both firms had strong, able management teams, and it was hard for either side to imagine ceding control to the other. Seemingly simple issues, such as which firm's name would come first in the merged organization, could not be resolved. Even more important was the matter of differing modes of ownership. "They are publicly owned, we are private," Olsen notes. "Deep down, if you analyze the matter, it is very difficult to put a public and a private company together when the public company has no practical way to go private and the private company does not want to go public."

In retrospect, the two firms faced little choice except to merge or become competitors. Both were seeking to participate more fully in the global marketplace and during the 1980s each began to invade the other's turf, creating friction. In the mid-1980s, Willis acquired two U.S.-based surplus lines brokerage firms, Global Special Risks in New Orleans and McAlear Associates in Grand Rapids, Michigan. Although not direct competitors of J&H, they represented Willis's first wholly owned presence in the United States — a fact noted by a trade publication, which surmised that "the grip might be loosening" between J&H and Willis. In 1987, J&H acquired a British reinsurance broker, Carter Brito e Cunha Ltd., now Johnson & Higgins Ltd. — J&H's first direct venture in England. Willis chairman Roger Elliott, Palmer's successor, would later call the acquisition "a real sore in the wound." That same year, Willis acquired Stewart Wrightson, a sizable British insurance broker with U.S. operations.

In Goldberg's opinion, the Stewart Wrightson acquisition marked "the beginning of the end" of the J&H-Willis relationship. "It wasn't the buying of the firm that hurt Johnson & Higgins, it was that we were never told a word about it in advance," he maintains. "I think we rightfully expected if Willis made a move of that magnitude we would have been consulted."

Events moved with lightning speed in the spring of 1990. In May, virtually the entire J&H senior management team — a total of nearly 50 directors and other senior executives — went to London for three days to increase the firm's visibility in that critical market. It was a huge and highly successful undertaking. The J&H representatives hosted 500 members of the London underwriting community at a cocktail party at Guild Hall, and they in turn were feted by Lloyd's at a black-tie dinner. The final night saw a "farewell dinner" for the boards of J&H and Willis at the Imperial War Museum, an ironic setting given the events that followed — and a "farewell" that would prove more permanent than expected.

Some two weeks later, Hatcher was in Paris on business when he received a phone call from Elliott, who said he wanted to get together to discuss an urgent matter. The two had become close personal friends in their quest to amalgamate the firms. Elliott asked Hatcher to stop by in London on his return flight to New York, but Hatcher demurred, telling Elliott, "I know it's bad news that you want to see me about. That's why I'm not anxious to just drop off in London and have you tweak my tail." Elliott agreed to fly to Paris the next morning to meet with Hatcher over breakfast. At that meeting, Elliott dropped a bombshell: Willis Faber planned to merge with Corroon & Black Corp., one of J&H's U.S. competitors.

That breakfast marked the end of one of the truly remarkable stories in the history of the insurance industry. A 98-year transatlantic alliance, based on little more than a handshake, had come to an abrupt conclusion. J&H and Willis could no longer work together, now that they were about to become direct competitors in the United States. Was Hatcher disappointed? "Yes, I was disappointed, but I certainly wasn't dejected," he says. Speaking of his desire to merge the two firms, he comments, "It's just something that didn't get done."

On the other hand, Olsen — who never favored a merger and who immediately considered Willis a direct competitor once its planned consolidation with Corroon & Black was revealed — takes a gloves-off attitude. Some Willis executives apparently believed their firm could remain in UNISON even after merging with Corroon & Black. Speaking of one Willis executive who expressed that view, Olsen says, "I was astounded that he was astounded that they were now out of UNISON."

"Did we ever say to ourselves, if we don't merge, at some point this relationship has to end?," Meyer remarks. "We never put it on the table that boldly. But we thought at some point something might happen."

BUILDING A LONDON OPERATION

Hatcher was in his final months as chairman and CEO when these events occurred. In December 1990, he retired as scheduled and was succeeded by Olsen.

On the day when Hatcher was meeting with Elliott in Paris, Olsen and Ken Hecken — then J&H president and vice chairman, respectively — were attending a meeting of the National Association of Insurance Brokers in Sea Island, Georgia. Olsen was about to join Hecken for some relaxation on the beach when he received a transatlantic phone call from Hatcher, informing him of the conversation with Elliott. "I went out to the beach and gave the news to Ken," Olsen says. "He assumed I was kidding, which I tend to do periodically. He said, 'Stop this. Let's talk about something serious.'" It took nearly ten minutes for Olsen to convince Hecken the news was true, after which they began to devise a plan of action. "We got out some paper and started writing down, What does it mean? What do we do?," according to Olsen. "We were sitting in beach chairs, and it was really kind of fun and exciting. We filled several sheets of paper with ideas."

One of the first priorities, they decided, was to communicate the J&H-Willis breakup to employees, UNISON partners and clients. Olsen returned to his office the next day and immediately held two open meetings in the J&H cafeteria for New York employees, explaining the "divorce" and answering questions. His talk and the Q&A were videotaped and shipped within a day to all J&H offices and UNISON partners around the world.

Meanwhile, J&H began examining its options for handling U.K. placements. Dick Meyer, one of the firm's top executives, was dispatched to London, where he would remain for a year and a half, supervising the transition as business was moved from Willis to J&H. Both firms pledged to keep the interests of clients uppermost as this occurred. No business was transferred from Willis to J&H without the client's approval.

"There were two components, wholesale and retail," Meyer explains. "We had an existing platform, Carter Brito, for the wholesale part. They were reinsurance brokers, but we had the immediate ability to put wholesale brokers into their office. I went over July 20, 1990. We made our first strategic hire on August 13, 1990, and went on from there. So that decision was made immediately."

However, J&H did not have a vehicle for its retail business, which continued to be serviced by Willis pending other arrangements — a point that did not escape other British brokers. Within a week, nearly a dozen British firms had contacted J&H to discuss acting as exclusive correspondent or to offer to be acquired. Rather than aligning itself with any of them, J&H opted to proceed carefully and methodically. First, Meyer and his colleagues analyzed 145 U.K. brokers, with the thought that J&H might affiliate with one. "We formed a 'change committee,' and that committee examined all those brokers," Meyer says. "We rated them on 17 different characteristics, and that process caused us to weed out a whole bunch. We ended up with approximately 20. We took a hard look at each of these firms, and one or more of us interviewed each one."

The change committee, led by Olsen, then narrowed the search to five firms, though for various reasons none really fit, including conflicting philosophies of expansion. "Many of the firms were interested in growth for growth's sake," Olsen explains. "But our clients don't care that much about size. They care about our ability to provide the best service."

Dick Nielsen says some people felt J&H was "painfully slow" in deciding what to do in London. "But we needed to make the right decision, not a quick decision," he says. "People seemed to forget that we had the luxury of time. Willis Faber was more than happy to continue handling our clients. So it wasn't as if our clients suffered a bit while we explored our options."

In late 1990, taking a new tack, J&H formed a small committee to reexamine its alternatives. In its report, titled "New Blokes on the Block," the committee recommended that J&H forget about acquiring a broker and build its own British operation from scratch. That recommendation was approved unanimously by the J&H board on April 19, 1991, and since then the firm has gone about establishing and developing a wholly owned London-based retail operation, Johnson & Higgins UK Ltd. Building from the ground up is expensive. However, by taking this approach, rather than acquiring, J&H has been able to instill its culture of teamwork and client service right from the start. "I think Johnson & Higgins made the right decision in not trying to acquire, because I firmly believe that nearly all London brokers have some skeleton in their closet," says Christian Dahms of UNISON partner Jauch & Hübener. "To start with a clean sheet of paper made a lot of sense."

Olsen expresses great enthusiasm for what J&H is doing in the United Kingdom today. Johnson & Higgins UK Ltd. has offices in London, Birmingham, Glasgow, Manchester, Newcastle and Reading, as well as in Dublin, Republic of Ireland. "We had a great relationship with Willis for many years," Olsen says, "but the time had come to move on." J&H was fortunate in its timing, he says. When the company began staffing its U.K. operation, the London insurance industry was in a slump and other firms weren't hiring. "As a result, we were able to hand-pick some of the best people in the City," he asserts.

Over 90 percent of the U.K. retail premium volume of J&H clients has now been transferred from Willis to Johnson & Higgins UK Ltd. The transfer of UNISON business from Willis to J&H Ltd. has proceeded on schedule, as well. Seeking out indigenous business is also part of the plan. In fact, many British corporations quickly expressed a desire to learn more about the new firm in town. "People want to see us, they want to hear about us," Meyer reported not long ago. "Are we getting some local business? Yes. Are we getting all we want? Not yet. But we will."

11.

U.S. Retail in the Pressure Cooker

United States retail is the bread and butter of Johnson & Higgins, accounting for over 60 percent of worldwide revenues. Retail refers to the day-to-day brokerage and consulting services provided by J&H to its corporate clients. It is a highly competitive business in the midst of exhilarating change — change which creates both challenge and opportunity.

"I can't think of another industry that's a more classic example of a service business," David Olsen says. "There are a lot of competitors, a handful of big ones and a zillion smaller ones. We can be fired at any point and if somebody can do it faster, cheaper, better, they'll be hired. Of course, if we can do it faster, cheaper, better, we'll be retained."

Or as Norman Barham puts it, "If we're the best, we'll do well. If not, we won't be around."

The challenge (and opportunity) faced by J&H is to understand and meet the needs of clients, control costs, and improve its profitability at a time when margins throughout the brokerage industry are under pressure. Joseph P. Platt, Jr., a J&H director, says, "Profit margins in retail brokerage have been dropping for 15 years. We want to get off that curve. We want to beat the market

Dick Nielsen, president and chief operating officer, heads U.S. retail operations and is a driving force in the J&H Quality initiative.

by differentiating ourselves. Different and better."

In fact, J&H has a long-standing record of profitable growth in retail brokerage, dating back to the firm's founding 150 years ago. Speaking of the company's strengths in retail, Olsen says, "There are a lot of good things going on at J&H — best people in the industry, great level of client service, a lot of new business, not much lost business, expansion around the world."

On the other hand, the market has never been more demanding than it is today. "The needs of our clients have changed dramatically in the past 10 years," says J&H president Dick Nielsen, who heads U.S. retail. "The transaction itself is important certainly. But the advice and counsel and other things we bring to the table have become so much more highly valued by clients than the transaction alone."

Gerald R. Swanson, J&H branch manager in Seattle, observes, "Years ago, we kept a client's business by knowing the right people, including the CEO. Relationships are still important, but the professionalism at all levels must be that much greater. And there is so much more specialization. For instance, in our office we have a geologist. He understands mines and the people involved in mines and we have developed a lot of business in that area."

COMPETITIVE BRAWL

With margins narrowing and client expectations increasing, an industry shakeout looms on the horizon. Johnson & Higgins intends to be a big winner. It has not backed away from the competitive brawl that is brewing in domestic retail brokerage.

The past few years have seen far-reaching change in the way the company meets the needs of clients and delivers retail services. In 1991, J&H reorganized its domestic retail branch system by dividing it into four regions, each headed by a director. The four directors report, in turn, to Nielsen. Previously, because different branches reported to different senior executives in a rather haphazard organizational structure, there was no single focus on investments or budgets. "This is an enormous change," Nielsen attests. "For the first time in recent memory, one person is responsible for U.S. retail operations." These operations include the firm's 52 domestic retail branches as well as the practice offices, target marketing groups, Johnson & Higgins Financial Services and the captive treaty business.

The person in charge is, of course, Nielsen. "I think what's exciting is that Dick has given some very strong leadership to the biggest component of Johnson & Higgins," says William C. Bauman, director in charge of the Southern Region. "Dick has successfully communicated to all the leaders of the retail operations his vision for this part of the company. That may seem like an ordinary event to outsiders, but in fact it was a singular event in our recent history. There is a sense now in retail of what we want to be and that we have a strong hand on the tiller." One of J&H's goals is to gain market share by increasing its domestic retail revenues at a compound annual rate of six percent and profits at a compound annual rate of 10 percent through 1998. In other words, J&H, already big, wants to get bigger. "The volume of business is real important," according to Barham. "The only way to have clout with the underwriters is to be a big player. The more money you put into the marketplace, the more clout you have."

To meet its objectives, J&H has stepped up its sales and marketing activities and expanded its employee training programs. Moreover, each of the four regions is developing innovative approaches. "One of the things we have done," Nielsen says, "is to push more and more decision-making into the regions and branches and get it out of New York." Twenty years ago, it was sacrosanct that each J&H domestic branch had to provide full services. The Central Region, for one, is now breaking that mold. Some services, such as marine brokerage, are being concentrated in larger offices in the region. In the Western Region, San Francisco is the first J&H office to be organized by industry groups, such as financial institutions, rather than by insurance disciplines, such as property insurance. "That was created here," says James D. Altman, the San Francisco branch manager. "We're a guinea pig, I believe, for J&H, because I think more offices will be moving in this direction."

Speaking of these and other developments, Nielsen says, "They're a sign of much more change coming down the road."

In addition, J&H director John V. Deitchman notes that "who does what" within the insurance industry is undergoing a profound transformation. "We are doing some of the things the client used to do," he says, "because we can do them cheaper and better. We are also moving into some of the things the underwriter did, and the underwriter is moving into some of the things we used to do. So the whole arrangement is changing." For instance, J&H is heavily involved in claims management — reviewing carriers' claims practices, modifying them where appropriate, establishing performance objectives and evaluating results. Obtaining the lowest premium rate is no longer the only yardstick in selecting an underwriter; factors such as claims processing are also given consideration. Going one step further, J&H is evaluating independent providers of claims services. "It's not just the carrier that might provide the claims handling now," Deitchman says. "It's who else is out there. In a sense, we're broking the claims handling piece, not just the transaction. Sometimes you separate those out."

Nielsen says, "Clients are continually asking us to do new and different things." In southern California, for instance, Jennifer Pierson of the J&H Costa Mesa branch now spends three days a week at the offices of Fluor Corporation as an extension of that company's risk management staff, providing her expertise on special projects. In that role, she deals not only with J&H but with other brokers on Fluor's behalf. "I think it was a good move on our part to offer that, and it just shows the commitment to service," she says.

In still another key move, J&H is strengthening its programs to serve mid-sized accounts. J&H has traditionally been number one in serving large corporations, but has been less powerful in the middle market. "We've been doing middle-market business for a long, long time," remarks Christine DiBona, a senior vice president in the Washington, D.C., office. "But in the past ten years we have become serious about it. In the past five years, we've become very, very serious about it and have committed tremendous resources." Middle-market accounts in the Washington area include government contractors, financial institutions, law firms and others. Nationwide, such accounts are served through the Insurance Services Division (ISD), which has professionals in each J&H office. Recently, ISD has formed partnerships with several leading underwriters to serve mid-sized accounts.

LEADING-EDGE USE OF TECHNOLOGY

With mock surprise, Nielsen exclaims, "I never thought I would see the day when J&H won an award for automation. We won the Smithsonian the first year of that award! And I said, 'We did what? Are you talking about the same J&H I know?'" In fact, leadership in the use of technology is a critical element of the firm's retail strategy.

Alan G. Page, J&H chief information officer and director, says the company began to increase its technology investments in the 1980s when it realized that the personal computer and other advances would have a significant impact on the brokerage business. "We either had to get this right or lose our franchise," he says. "Our goal in using technology is to leverage as much information as we can to help our clients solve their problems."

As exemplified by the prestigious Computer World-Smithsonian Award, captured by J&H in 1993 for its powerful J&H InfoEdge communications system, Johnson & Higgins has taken the technology lead in the brokerage industry. Indeed, few recent developments at J&H are more compelling than InfoEdge, an on-line system which allows J&H brokers worldwide to share information via their desk-top computers. Warming to the subject, Nielsen asserts, "We have changed the way people work. We have changed the availability and flow of information on a two-way basis."

Developed in-house on Lotus Notes, J&H InfoEdge includes an array of standard features, such as E-Mail and fax. It is the special features, however, that set the system apart and make it such an effective device for managing the firm's retail brokerage business. Using InfoEdge, a broker in any J&H office can query the company's entire team of professionals for ideas and advice. A recent request came from a broker in Pittsburgh who was establishing a captive to reinsure a client's directors and officers liability coverage. He wanted to know whether others had established such companies and, if so, whether they had any particular cautions or advice. In the past, according to William W. Wilson III, senior vice president, the Pittsburgh broker might have sought advice by contacting one of the company "gurus" in New York. "But you were always going to those same people, and the world doesn't revolve around New York," he adds. InfoEdge allows brokers to draw on the expertise of the entire company to get the best possible information and ideas. "The system permits you to create a 'virtual' team of people all over the world who contribute to solving a problem," Wilson reports. "It's amazing to see this happen."

In the case of the Pittsburgh broker, within two days he had received replies from six J&H brokers across the U.S. and in Bermuda. These replies (on line in InfoEdge for any J&H broker to see) in turn prompted comments from others nationwide, resulting in a lively multiparty discussion of the merits, technical aspects and recent J&H experiences in employing captives for D&O liability coverage.

At any given time, dozens of inquiries on various topics are active in InfoEdge. The system is workable because inquiries are categorized by topic, such as type of insurance and industry group of the client. A broker in Los Angeles, for instance, with expertise in pollution liability insurance could automatically track all questions related to that topic. Or a broker in Detroit could view all inquiries related to vehicle manufacturers.

Why would a J&H broker in, say, Seattle take time to respond to a question from a broker in Pittsburgh? One reason is that J&H brokers are expected to support the firm's culture of teamwork. Wilson points out, also, that responding to inquiries offers a tremendous opportunity for brokers to gain visibility within the company.

Henry Ward Johnson & Co.

Founded in 1989, Henry Ward Johnson & Company, Inc., is "a whole series of little things which, when you add them up, are a very big thing," according to Rufus J. Williams III, who heads the J&H subsidiary. The company has approximately 350 employees and is headquartered in New York. Describing his operation as being "very entrepreneurial," Williams says his group "began with a vision" of bringing together various wholesale businesses that already existed within J&H and developing others.

Henry Ward Johnson participates in three main businesses: wholesale brokerage and facultative reinsurance, association and affinity programs, and industry group profit centers. "What ties it all together?," Williams asks. "Well, it's not retail brokerage, it's not employee benefits consulting and it's not treaty reinsurance. Therefore, it's Henry Ward Johnson."

Apart from its wholesale brokerage operations, the company is primarily a developer of products that Williams views as being "niches or orphans." Products are sold mainly through retail brokers, including J&H. One example is the company's comprehensive property and casualty program offered to non-profit nursing and retirement facilities that are members of the American Association of Homes for the Aging. Another is its bank master trust program. The bank product is a highly automated program that provides property and casualty insurance for trust departments and trust officers in the handling of physical assets held in trust. "What really builds our business is great ideas and market relationships," Williams states.

He adds, "Successful brokerage companies for the future will be those that have a knowledge base in all facets of the business and have the commercial moxie to find opportunities and translate them into profits and growth." Henry Ward Johnson will continue to play a key role in developing new businesses for J&H and meeting the changing needs of clients.

Above, J&H InfoEdge won the prestigious Computer World-Smithsonian Award. InfoEdge gives J&H brokers instantaneous access to a wealth of information and allows them to communicate with colleagues around the world. Below right, J&H's STARS software helps companies control their workers' compensation costs.

InfoEdge includes an "administrative views" feature that allows Nielsen and other senior executives to monitor the rich interchange of ideas that takes place daily on InfoEdge.

Besides this market assistance feature, InfoEdge provides on-line access to hundreds of databases — many proprietary to J&H — to help brokers in their work. Moreover, J&H is beginning to use InfoEdge to go on-line with clients. "By 1998," Nielsen says, "we anticipate that 75 percent of our large clients will be connected electronically to their J&H team."

STARS AND OTHER PROPRIETARY SOFTWARE

There is another vital facet of J&H's technology strategy: perhaps surprisingly, the company has become the leading provider of risk management software for corporations. In support of the company's retail client relationships, software is written by a team of some 35 J&H programmers. "We're not in the software business," Nielsen cautions, "although in a narrow sense maybe we are. These are programs that help clients deal with their risk problems."

Robert G. Petrie III, J&H vice president, notes that J&H began writing software programs in the late 1980s in response to three trends: the power and flexibility of personal computers, the growth of self-insurance, and the upward spiral of clients' medical and litigation costs. "We were focusing on new products that weren't necessarily in the business of placing insurance," he relates. "We looked at these three trends and saw a hole big enough to drive a truck through."

J&H's initial success was STARS, introduced in 1990 and used today by some 300 corporations. STARS enables companies to monitor their workers' compensation costs and isolate problem areas quickly and efficiently. J&H not only sells the software, but helps companies analyze the findings. Since then, J&H has introduced software programs to: help companies with numerous similar facilities, such as franchise food chains, reduce their liability exposures; allow companies to compile property values, construction information and other data in an effective format for presentation to underwriters; and permit large decentralized multinational companies to track and analyze their worldwide insurance policies. Sophisticated new programs are in the works, including ones which will allow companies to compare their risk costs against industry-specific benchmarks.

Petrie says the company's strong effort in software development highlights a fundamental trend of the brokerage business — away from buying insurance per se, toward solving clients' problems. "The way we look at the world today," he says, "is not, 'how do we buy insurance,' but 'how do we structure deals that are a combination of insurance and noninsurance to arrive at the best solution for you, the client.'"

As we shall see in the next chapter, another fundamental way in which J&H is differentiating itself — and seeking to address the changing needs of clients — is through its companywide Quality initiative.

12.

"If We're the Best, Why Do We Have to Change?"

As we have seen, there have been several important turning points in Johnson & Higgins' history. Will Quality be another turning point, as J&H seeks to meet the changing needs of clients and improve its profitability in today's highly competitive global marketplace?

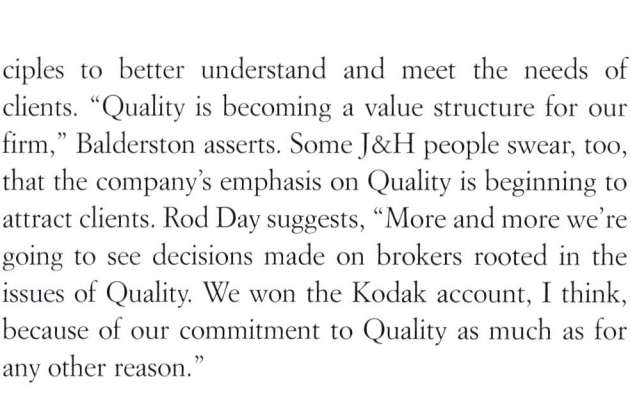

J&H began its Quality initiative in 1991, prompting many employees to ask, "If we're the best, why do we have to change?" Elizabeth J. Balderston, who chairs the J&H Quality task force, acknowledges there was initial skepticism. However, with the program now in its fourth year, reservations have largely melted away and Quality has gained widespread support as a better way to run the company. In fact, J&H president Dick Nielsen sees Quality as "the single most important thing this firm has done, is doing, will do." He adds, "We have the opportunity, done right, to dramatically differentiate ourselves from the competition."

Quality is already having an impact — from little things, like phones at many offices being answered after fewer rings, to big things, such as the use of Quality principles to better understand and meet the needs of clients. "Quality is becoming a value structure for our firm," Balderston asserts. Some J&H people swear, too, that the company's emphasis on Quality is beginning to attract clients. Rod Day suggests, "More and more we're going to see decisions made on brokers rooted in the issues of Quality. We won the Kodak account, I think, because of our commitment to Quality as much as for any other reason."

Encouragement from Clients

"Quality" has been a catchword in American industry for nearly a decade. As practiced by many companies, it embraces such concepts as employee empowerment, focus on the customer, teamwork and continuous improvement. Spurred to become a Quality company by several clients (notably GTE Corporation) and a number of employees (including William L. Bradford, who managed the Johnson & Johnson account and kept plugging away for months on the topic), J&H decided that its initiative would be about change. Christine LaSala says, "We recognized that Quality was a useful word around which to rally, but in fact we were talking about a basic change in the way we manage our business and serve our clients."

J&H began by appointing a Quality task force headed by LaSala. Over a six-month period in 1991, task force members interviewed approximately 120 larger clients, many middle-market clients, some ex-clients and more than 200 Johnson & Higgins employees to determine what clients want from a broker, how well J&H was meeting their needs and whether any internal impediments thwarted J&H people from serving clients effectively.

The results were surprising, even shocking, for a firm that has long prided itself on being the best. "We found that something wasn't quite right, that we weren't delivering the level of service clients thought we should," says James D. Appleton, a task force member and head of J&H University. Clients described J&H as a highly capable broker. However, being proficient in placing insurance and other basics of risk management consulting was no longer enough. "The marketplace was changing and we needed to change too," Appleton states.

The interviews confirmed that a fundamental shift in the business environment had major implications for insurance brokers. Corporate staffs were being stretched thin, doing more with less, using brokers as a staff extension. Risk management issues were moving into the highest levels of corporate management and being viewed increasingly in the context of overall financial strategies. Many companies were seeking to form strategic alliances with their suppliers.

In the survey, many clients expressed a desire for a breadth and depth of brokerage service that neither J&H nor any other broker was providing. "Are we good listeners? Do we take enough time to understand a client's business? Do we advise rather than sell? The answer was no, no, no," according to LaSala. Dan Knise, a task force member from the Washington, D.C., office says, "The survey showed that people who had been our clients the longest thought less of our service than newer clients. That was disturbing." On the other hand, no broker was consistently fulfilling client expectations.

The task force concluded that J&H had an opportunity to set itself apart by delivering the more demanding and meaningful level of service that clients were calling for and no one was providing.

Creating and Implementing a Plan

The client interviews conducted in 1991 put J&H and its marketplace under the microscope and provided the basis for developing a Quality program. As Nielsen points out, "It's easy to talk about change in the abstract, but we needed a practical framework for implementing Quality and bringing about personal change."

The program, as designed by the task force, embodies four major goals for change:

Strengthen client focus – Clearly understanding what a client, external or internal, wants and values is the starting point for meeting that client's needs.

Enhance skills – Meeting the client's needs requires also that J&H'ers have more consultative skills, such as questioning, listening, problem solving and work planning.

Master teamwork – Clients want J&H people to work in teams to develop meaningful solutions. In today's complex business environment, one person alone cannot find the best answers.

Measure and improve performance – Clients care about results, not actions. Results can be improved only if they are measurable.

The Five Major Themes

WHAT OUR CLIENTS WANT

1. UNDERSTAND MY BUSINESS

Clients expect us to learn and to know their business and their industry; they expect us to become better able to identify risk issues over time. In addition, clients clearly look to us to ask probing questions so as to reveal their _wants_ and issues of concern to them.

2. FORM A PARTNERSHIP WITH ME

We're expected to treat clients as carefully as we treat our prospects; we're expected to work closely with the client to accomplish mutual objectives. But clients _want_ more than that. They _want_ us continuously to improve the impact of that partnership by adapting to each other's changing needs and wants. They _want_ J&H to build ever higher levels of trust and candor.

3. ADVISE, DON'T JUST SELL

Clients expect us to provide excellent, cost-effective brokering services and to harness our market knowledge and clout for their benefit. At the same time, clients — again and again — _want_ us to listen first, and then to offer them advice and counsel. And they _want_ us to develop innovative, relevant solutions for them.

4. OFFER A *TEAM* OF QUALITY PEOPLE

Clients expect a strong relationship with their primary account manager. They expect us to possess solid skills and to demonstrate a deep commitment to them. Beyond that, clients _want_ J&H to serve them through a _team_ of Quality people — a team that brings together the needed resources and expertise to offer ideas and solutions.

5. PAY ATTENTION TO THE DAY-TO-DAY

Today's clients expect us to respond promptly to their needs, to have a real sense of urgency. They expect us to deliver relevant, accurate, and timely products. They expect us to keep them informed of pertinent market developments. In addition, what clients _want_ is that we anticipate what's needed and that we know why it's needed.

Research that led to the Quality initiative identified five major client "wants."

Today, Quality is being spread throughout the firm by teams of three to ten task force members. Each team is like an itinerant university taking the teaching of Quality right to the branches. The task force currently consists of 43 employees who continue in their regular assignments while devoting approximately 30 percent of their time to the Quality initiative.

"We're moving slowly, but it's the right way to succeed," Nielsen says. "We don't simply throw a bunch of corporate manuals at the branch. A team of people goes into each branch to help our employees understand what we're trying to accomplish. We provide some education, some training, but after six months the branch is expected to assume ownership."

Three Directions

The Quality program is being driven toward its four goals from three directions:

Top-down – "If David Olsen doesn't buy into Quality, it ain't gonna happen," David F. Peck of J&H Stamford noted several months ago. In fact, Olsen and other senior executives have participated in Questioning and Active Listening training and Team-Based Problem Solving. In some cases, they are forming teams to solve problems, such as an Olsen-led team charged with better communicating J&H's vision, values and direction.

Sideways – This involves efforts that cut across the business units of the company. A recent example is the redesign of the employee hiring, development, evaluation and compensation systems to improve J&H's ability to attract, train, reward and keep qualified people.

Bottom-up – "Bottom-up" encompasses an array of activities in the branches and business units, focused on professional skills, teamwork and client service. "We start with core skill training and move to doing 'real work' together as soon as possible," says task force member Lyn S. Kelley of J&H Cleveland.

One of the key activities in the branches is a formal process of dialogues with clients. These dialogues — based on the principles of listening, sharing expectations and probing to understand a client's particular needs — represent a major cultural shift. "We're teaching our people the consultative process of discovering with the client what they want and value," Balderston says. The end result is a written performance plan which is developed jointly with the client and shared with the entire J&H team involved with the account. "It used to be that only the account manager and maybe the key broker understood the overall service targets," Balderston says. "So an internal outcome of Quality is broader knowledge within J&H of what the client wants and values. As a member of the team, I can now answer the client's questions and respond quickly because I know what the client wants and am focused on the plan."

Another major element is the identification and redesign of internal processes to make them more efficient and effective. The Quality initiative encourages team-based problem solving and "performance breakthrough projects" — steps a branch can take to achieve quick, meaningful results. Not long ago, Rod Day noted, "There are lots of things we can do in that basic blocking and tackling arena — such as, in Stamford, answering the telephone within two rings and getting the caller into the hands of someone who knows the account 75 percent of the time the first time. Clients are already telling us they see a difference." Another branch achieved an 80 percent reduction in turnaround time for routine correspondence. There are hundreds of similar examples throughout the branch system.

Nielsen stresses that Quality is not a separate project or an end unto itself, but is being woven into the daily fabric of the way the company conducts its business. "Our challenge is to change and at the same time preserve the best of J&H," he remarks.

Susan M. Sauer of J&H Chicago adds, "Quality is here to stay not because management tells us we must live this way. It's here to stay because it is so personally fulfilling. I have more skills and feel more confident in serving my clients. And I'm getting more feedback on how well I'm doing. The first winner is the individual."

13.

David Olsen: Why He Defies the Status Quo

On first meeting David Olsen, one quickly realizes just how much he relishes his work. A smile spreads across his face as he relates "some of the things I think about" — vision (is Johnson & Higgins on the right track?), profits (how can the company increase them?), ownership (should the ownership profile of J&H change?), opportunities (what are they and how can J&H capitalize on them?), creativity (how can J&H and its people be more innovative and entrepreneurial?), size (how big is big enough?), structure (how does J&H keep changing its structure to be efficient and competitive?), meritocracy (how can J&H better identify and reward its true performers?), competitors (who will they be in the future?), and on and on. The enthusiasm is contagious.

The 57-year-old Olsen has been chairman and chief executive officer of Johnson & Higgins since 1990, when he succeeded Bob Hatcher. Although he doesn't use these particular words, it is clear that Olsen thinks he has one of the best jobs in the world.

Olsen is a shirt-sleeve executive. "It is certainly my style to be informal," he says. "People work better and are happier under those circumstances." Like many J&H'ers, he puts in long hours. He usually arrives at the office at 7:15 a.m., leaves by 5:30 p.m. and often attends early-evening nonprofit board meetings. He generally dines with clients or business associates before heading home, sometimes to work some more. His wife, Bobbie, frequently joins him at client dinners, and he often discusses business with her. "She knows a lot of what goes on and is a good sounding board," he says.

(When their two children were growing up, Olsen balanced career and family responsibilities by catching the 6 a.m. train to the office. That way, he could head back home promptly at 5 p.m. and spend time with the kids in the evening. After the children went to bed, he often pulled out his briefcase and completed the day's assignments. "It's funny," he says, "both of our kids, who are now in their late 20s, mentioned that they had never realized I worked hard. They just assumed I was lolling around. How nice!")

For relaxation, he enjoys tennis, scuba diving and skiing. He played on his high school golf team and is thinking of taking up the sport again. He also was an Eagle Scout and still likes to hike to keep in shape.

Collegial Management Style

Olsen is a conceptual thinker who enjoys eliciting the viewpoints of others and challenging the status quo. "I think David has opened J&H to more startling change than any leader," Chris LaSala declares. "He has permitted a very dynamic environment."

Director John W. Gussenhoven observes, "His style is open. He will listen to anybody who has something constructive to contribute. I think he's consensus-oriented. He tends to talk out where he's heading on certain decisions before making those decisions in order to hear the views of others."

Christian Dahms of UNISON partner Jauch & Hübener has worked with the past three chief executives of Johnson & Higgins — Dick Purnell, Bob Hatcher and David Olsen. He points out that each has had a different personality and has espoused his own distinct management style. "I admire the company's way of doing this," Dahms says. "If it is always the same type of man, you are in jeopardy of remaining what you used to be 25 years ago. To change the leadership gives you an almost automatic guarantee that you are going to move forward, because each new leader shakes up the organization the way he thinks it should be."

Speaking of Olsen, Dahms says, "He is a very demanding person. Nothing wrong with that. In the international context of the various UNISON issues, he says, in my view, a little too often what is in it for Johnson & Higgins. But again, nothing wrong with that. He's a good sport. He has a terrific sense of humor. A great man to work with." Compared with Hatcher, known for his southern charm and his proclivity for cementing business ties by establishing personal friendships, Dahms views Olsen as "more the cool-type business person who keeps relationships on a professional level."

Director's Son

Born in New York in 1937, Olsen grew up with Johnson & Higgins in his blood. His father, Alexander Olsen, spent 46 years with the company, joining J&H out of high school as a mail clerk while continuing his education at night to earn a bachelor's degree from New York University. Through persistence and hard work, Alexander Olsen rose steadily within the firm, serving for a time as Detroit branch manager and eventually becoming a director before retiring in 1962. Olsen says his father "talked endlessly about the company, it was his whole life." Listening to these conversations at the dinner table, young David wondered why insurance

David Olsen has brought a more collegial management style to J&H since his election as chief executive officer in 1990.

broking didn't sound like more fun. Although David and his father were close, David had no thought of joining Johnson & Higgins when he grew up.

On graduating from Bowdoin College in Maine, Olsen spent a year with the Great American Insurance Company prior to military service. That one year proved to be a revelation. "During that one-year training program I became fascinated with the insurance industry," he says. He returned to Great American following a tour of duty as an officer in the U.S. Army Transportation Corps and, despite being recruited by J&H, stayed with Great American "because I felt I had a great career going." In 1966, Dick Henshaw of J&H approached Olsen with a job offer as a marine account executive in the San Francisco office, and this time Olsen said yes.

The San Francisco office at the time was a "classic example of the old style of authoritarian leadership at J&H," Olsen says. He recalls an especially horrid example. About a week after he had joined the office, a veteran employee invited him on a sales call to the president of a dredging company. The employee opened the meeting by saying to the president, "We're from Johnson & Higgins and surely you know about Johnson & Higgins," to which the executive replied that he didn't but would be glad to learn. Olsen continues, "And this may seem hard to believe, but the J&H person said, 'Well, if you've never heard of Johnson & Higgins you're probably not the type of company we would do business with anyway.' And with that he said thank you and we left. When we got back to the office, I thought, 'This is nuts.' I knew Johnson & Higgins wasn't like that. So I called the president of the prospect company and said, 'I'm calling to apologize, but I'm also calling to tell you this is not the way J&H normally operates.' And he sort of laughed and said, 'Thanks for calling, but don't come and see me again.'"

"That was the old school," Olsen emphasizes. "We would never tolerate that kind of behavior today."

By 1971, Olsen felt his career was stymied. The people above him were not scheduled to retire for years, and there seemed no prospect of his advancing until they did. Dick Mittnacht, a director based in New York, was searching for someone to take charge of the Chicago Marine Department, which was not performing well, and asked Henry Cabaud, the San Francisco branch manager, about Olsen. Olsen recalls, "Cabaud told him, 'Forget it. He loves San Francisco. His wife's from California. He's doing a great job. Why would he ever leave?'" But Mittnacht persisted and approached Olsen directly, discovering that he welcomed the opportunity. "It's a good lesson not to assume you know what people want to do with their careers," Olsen says.

Moving to Chicago, Olsen found the office's Marine Department to be in disarray and proceeded to replace nearly all its personnel, rapidly improving its performance. Six years later, in 1977, hoping to become a branch manager, Olsen ran into a roadblock. John McEown, now retired as executive vice president of J&H, picks up the story: "I was sent out by Dick Purnell from New York to look after Chicago on an interim basis after Jack Dowling, the resident partner, took disability and had to stop work. That was very unexpected and there was no one there we could see to step in and take over the office right away." Over the next few months, three employees in Chicago — one being Olsen — emerged as candidates to head the branch. In effect, they competed for the top spot by running the office jointly under McEown's supervision. "I became close to David," McEown says, "and recognized his very superior people skills and his great commitment to the business and his creativity." McEown therefore recommended Olsen for the job. However, Purnell decided to bring in an employee from another office. Olsen, then 40, was clearly disappointed about being passed over, but as fate would have it, he did not have to wait long.

Shortly thereafter, Palmer Sparkman, manager of the Houston office, died tragically of a heart attack at age 42 while jogging on New Year's Day 1979, and Olsen was chosen as his successor. Finally getting an opportunity to run a branch, Olsen earned high marks by increasing the revenues and profits of the Houston office even after the Texas oil economy went into a tailspin. One year after being named branch manager, he was elected to the J&H board, and five years after that, in 1985, was transferred to New York as executive vice president and Hatcher's heir-apparent. Traditionally, J&H chairmen had hand-picked their successors, but Hatcher opened the choice to a vote of the board. Olsen believes his experience as a broker, client leader and department and branch manager was a definite asset in his being elected.

"When I came to New York, Bob Hatcher said to me, 'You've learned J&H from the bottom up, now learn it from the top down,'" Olsen says. Olsen was elected president and chief operating officer in 1987 and succeeded Hatcher as CEO in 1990.

A STILL-REMEMBERED SPEECH

"David was brand-new in New York, and we were having a meeting of the non-director branch managers," McEown recounts. "He had been one of that group and this was his first experience on the other side of the table. David had to help me preside over the formal dinner that ended the meetings. He felt it was important to make a good presentation. He came to me that afternoon and said very quietly, 'Can you help me? I've got a problem. I'd like to say something fun and clever, but my mind is a blank.' I said, 'Gee whiz, David, I'm not terribly creative at that sort of thing and I don't know what to tell you.' And then I said, 'Look, you don't have to be a stand-up comedian. Just compose a few thoughts. You don't have to be terribly profound, just be sincere.'" McEown heard no more about the matter and had no idea what Olsen was going to say until the moment arrived. "He got up and gave one of the best talks I've ever heard," McEown relates. "He had made all kinds of notes from the conference, and he brought them with him and gave an extemporaneous, very comical presentation of what we had been talking about for three days. Just absolutely brought the house down. That's David. Quick mind, very creative, terrific in front of an audience."

"SO DAMN DEMOCRATIC"

On becoming CEO, Olsen sought to establish a more inclusive style of management. Hatcher had initially embraced such a style when he was elected CEO, but had turned away from it over time. Hatcher himself says, "There have been different styles of men who have run this company, and I guess each one was good for his time. When my turn came, I thought management should be more collegial than it had been, that maybe decisions should be made upon the advice of some three or four or five of the most senior people, not made by the chairman, period. And then maybe it became too collegial. We got bogged down in collegiality, we got bogged down in committees. That almost wore me out. So then I reverted back to being a little bit more of a despot, I guess."

Dick Nielsen comments, "David really has opened up this process. He has opened up decisions to discussion, to debate, to different opinions, and I think it has been very healthy."

To be sure, the company is not managed by the full board of directors with each member having an equal vote. To do so, Rod Day says, would "paralyze" the firm. However, the executive committee, which currently has 13 members, meets monthly, "and David uses that forum to discuss strategic issues, investments, any other matters he wants to air," according to Day.

Olsen recalls a recent conversation with Dick Purnell. "I phoned him to ask for some ideas on a staff compensation problem," Olsen says, "and we had an interesting conversation. Basically he said, 'You know your problem? The reason you don't have any time to do anything is you are so damn democratic.' He was partially kidding, of course."

Addressing Important Issues of Change

As CEO, Olsen devotes much of his energy to positioning the company for the far-reaching changes sweeping through the insurance brokerage industry. Looking back over the past decade, since he first moved up into the ranks of J&H senior management, he says, "We've continued the rapid transition of J&H from an old club, operating relatively simply in an innately profitable industry, to a disciplined and sophisticated company, competing successfully in a very competitive and far less profitable business, by keeping what's good and by changing what's weak."

He lists some of the things that haven't changed at J&H during his five years as CEO:

- It has maintained its industry ranking of third largest broker in the United States and fifth in the world, without going public or borrowing money to do so.
- It has preserved a balance between short-term profits and long-term growth, collegial decision-making and speedy decisiveness, and the good attributes of a "club" and the need to be a modern corporation.
- The Johnson & Higgins name and reputation have been kept "high in the minds of movers and shakers."
- The company has continued its active program of community support, through contributions of both time and money.
- J&H has remained "a satisfying, exciting and rewarding place to work."

Olsen also cites some of the things that *have* changed at Johnson & Higgins:

- In the "people" area, he notes expanded opportunities for women, introduction of the Quality initiative, increased training activities (including the recent formation of J&H University, which embodies the concept of career-long education) and improved internal communication.
- On the global front, he cites acquisitions of equity interests in UNISON correspondents in the Netherlands, Spain, Portugal, Mexico and Sweden, expansion of the UNISON presence in Belgium, and the opening of J&H offices in China, Korea and other markets. In London, J&H is successfully building a company-owned business following the termination of its 98-year relationship with Willis Faber.
- With the addition of 19 managing principals (a new category of J&H shareholders), the firm has more owners than ever. The number of J&H people who own shares will continue to increase, opening greater opportunities for equity participation by employees.
- "Efficiency" is another major area of challenge and change. The company is "doing more with fewer people." Automation and "bureaucracy busting" have helped.
- Major business and investment opportunities have been pursued, including sponsorship of Global Capital Reinsurance Limited, a catastrophe property insurance company in Bermuda, and the recent joint purchase of the company's headquarters building at 125 Broad Street in New York with co-tenant Sullivan & Cromwell. "We looked at other opportunities, such as buying or merging with a big competitor, and wisely didn't act," he says.
- "We fixed what needed to be fixed," such as the sale of the company's Sibson & Company compensation consulting subsidiary and improvements in the performance of A. Foster Higgins & Co.
- As a result of a major new strategic planning program, Q:TAP, "we know more about ourselves than ever before." Moreover, the strategic plan establishes clear financial aspirations for the company into the next century.

Under the J&H bylaws, Olsen is scheduled to retire in 1997. "The firm is healthy and growing," he comments, "profits are stronger and I believe that J&H will be a better company when my term is over."

Employee Benefits Consulting

Johnson & Higgins entered the employee benefits consulting business in 1927, well before most other firms. With its early start, the company was well-equipped for the tremendous growth in group life, pensions, health insurance, profit sharing and other employee benefit programs that occurred in the years following World War II. Walter Clemens joined the Employee Benefits Department in 1954 as the 30th employee and recalls, "It was a demanding time, a demanding group, with change all about us." The department was headed for many years by Mort Denker, a brilliant, high-strung executive who was known as a tough boss but also had a terrific sense of humor. "Mort was tremendously bright, quick, aggressive," Clemens says. "Nobody talked about type A's back then, but that clearly was Mort. He drove hard and he drove for quality."

"The development of our employee benefit business was distinctly different from that of our competition," Ed Knetzger points out. Unlike other firms, many of which viewed benefits consulting as a loss leader for insurance brokerage, Denker insisted that J&H charge for its services and market them independently. Because benefits consulting was an important and growing business at J&H, the company attracted an exceptional group of benefits professionals. In fact, a number of them, including Clemens, Knetzger, Ric Johnson and John McEown, went on to become senior J&H executives.

The Employee Benefits Department grew and prospered through the 1970s before hitting on some hard times in the 1980s. McEown explains, "What went wrong was our failure to understand the competitive changes that were going on within the industry." While the benefits consulting business had traditionally been dominated by insurance brokers, actuarial consultants were now aggressively expanding their presence and charging for their services on a fee rather than a commission basis. "The more these firms grew, the more we settled into what we were doing," according to McEown. "The more they talked about the need to have a fee-based consultant, the more we sold the advantage of having a commission-based broker who could also do consulting." By the early 1980s, "benefits was still growing at a good pace and we were still making good money, but looking down the road you could see it wasn't going to last," McEown says.

In 1987, J&H retained McKinsey & Company to assess its benefits consulting business and recommend changes. "McKinsey concluded that we were trying to be all things to all people and the marketplace was confused as to our role," says J&H director Robert F. Powell, Jr. "We needed to redefine our business based on client needs and wants."

Out of that study came a top-to-bottom reorganization. A new wholly owned subsidiary, A. Foster Higgins & Co., Inc., was established to provide fee-based benefits consulting to large clients — services which had previously resided in each of the J&H retail branches but were now spun off into a separate corporation. The subsidiary was named after one of J&H's founders "because we felt we needed a name that had some tie to our parent company but also indicated we were independent," Powell states. In addition, an Employee Benefits Services group was created to meet the needs of middle-market accounts, and Johnson & Higgins Financial Services, Inc., was formed to manage a number of specialized insurance products.

The initial impact of the changes has been positive. "We're pleased with the overall growth rate of our combined benefit business and feel we've come a long way since the changes of the late 80s," Powell says. However, the benefits consulting business has become more complex and competitive than ever. "The face of the benefits marketplace is evolving right before our eyes," Powell says. He cites such examples as the consolidation of health care systems, the trend for corporations to outsource their human resources administration and rapid advances in technology. Also, the benefits consulting business is beginning to grow rapidly in many countries outside the United States as these countries privatize their pension and health care programs.

Foster Higgins is picking its opportunities carefully. "We are not on a mission to be the biggest, but we want to be the best in the markets we serve," Powell reports. He sees a major opportunity, for instance, to establish a leadership position in managed care consulting. Foster Higgins professionals are working closely with J&H professionals to solve client problems, such as managing workers' compensation costs. Where appropriate, the company is also seeking strategic alliances to enter new businesses.

"We all recognize that the growth rates of our core businesses won't match the past," Powell says. "Government legislation is no longer driving demand the way it used to, and the market has become more competitive than ever. To succeed, we have to be quick, smart and flexible and make sure we have the best people."

Johnson & Higgins has used various logotypes over the years. Among those shown here, the globe is the earliest. At the bottom is the current logo.

14.

Johnson & Higgins... A Celebration of People

Few companies that existed in 1845 are still in business today. Johnson & Higgins is a notable exception. Why has Johnson & Higgins grown and prospered when so many others have faltered along the way? The answer is people. At its heart, the company's 150-year history is a story of people working together to meet the needs of clients and constantly adapt to change.

In this book, we have met just a few of the highly skilled people who have made Johnson & Higgins the premier firm it is today. There are — and have been — countless more, dedicated to the firm's never-changing principles of professionalism, integrity and client service.

"Working as a team, with no individual star taking all the credit, that's the wonderful thing about Johnson & Higgins," says Roberta Davis, a senior vice president in Los Angeles.

"I don't know of another firm with more unsung heroes," John Keyser, director in charge of the Chicago office, comments. "We have succeeded and prospered through the efforts of thousands of people at all levels, not just a few at the top."

J&H people are self-starters who often go to great lengths to find innovative solutions or develop new business opportunities.

A number of years ago, Charles "Chic" Bertolacci in Seattle was approached by a client with a particular problem: the client was leasing aircraft to companies in foreign countries; insurance was not available to protect against political risk, such as confiscation of aircraft by foreign governments. Bertolacci and his team developed a specialized product, aviation political risk insurance, which is now used worldwide.

In Houston, Al Hyman saw that government agencies were not being well served by their brokers. J&H had traditionally shied away from this market, but Hyman and his team recognized the opportunities and established the J&H GovernmentGroup, which today is a nationwide force in insurance brokerage services for government entities.

Thirty years ago in Los Angeles, a young employee named Tip Geisbush convinced local J&H management to begin a program of cold sales calls. More than 3,500 calls were made in the first year without gaining a single new client. But Geisbush persisted and won a small new account, Toyota, which was just beginning to sell its cars in the United States. Toyota's imports grew, and soon J&H Los Angeles was serving other Japanese auto manufacturers as well. Today, J&H Los Angeles is the dominant broker in this major market segment, providing dedicated resources to meet the car companies' special needs.

In Chicago, Sue Sauer is developing a practice specialty in workers' compensation, helping clients find innovative solutions to soaring workers' comp costs.

Multinational corporations can now have seamless global property coverage, thanks to an idea conceived and executed by a team that includes Norman Barham, Mike Linde, Rob Meyers and Bob Schneider in New York and Howard Whitmore in Stamford, Connecticut. J&H global programs tie together worldwide insurance, service and automation in a single package, giving corporations greater consistency and control.

Karen Logue, originally from the Pittsburgh office and now in New York, and Sandy Berkowitz of Philadelphia, both of whom are nurse-attorneys, have been instrumental in building Johnson & Higgins' health care practice. The J&H HealthGroup serves the risk management needs of hospitals, doctor groups and other clients in the health care industry.

Darby Duryea and his team in New York, Bermuda and London developed an insurance facility to help shipowners satisfy the U.S. Coast Guard's financial requirements for vessels entering U.S. waters. The First Line program, introduced in 1994, is a fixed-cost facility that complements existing property and indemnity coverage and allows shipowners to budget costs absolutely.

Throughout the branches and around the world, similar examples of client service and entrepreneurship abound. David Olsen says, "We have always been committed to recruiting and keeping the best people, giving them the tools to do their best and then getting out of their way."

The future holds both challenge and opportunity. All insurance brokers will be under pressure to perform continuously better and keep pace with clients' changing needs. In this competitive battle, Johnson & Higgins has a not-so-secret weapon: its 8,400 people and the 6,000 people of its UNISON partners.

Olsen makes clear that "we have no desire to be the biggest, but we do intend to remain very big — and the best." Talented, motivated, highly skilled people, working together toward common goals, will continue to make the difference for Johnson & Higgins and its clients.

* * *

For 150 years, against passing fads and changing business currents, Johnson & Higgins has resolutely stood for the principles of professionalism and integrity. Today, J&H is quick to embrace the future while remaining true to the best of its past — a powerful combination as it begins its second 150 years.

BOARD OF DIRECTORS AS OF YEAR-END 1994

Seated, from left to right:

Joseph D. Roxe
John P. Keyser
Robert F. Powell, Jr.
James D. Altman
Thomas G. Patzau
Albert S. McGhee
David A. Olsen
Richard A. Nielsen
David W. Bianchi
E. Massie Valentine
Brian R. Hall
Gardner M. Mundy
Rodney D. Day III
Norman Barham

Standing, from left to right:

Joseph P. Platt, Jr.
Richard E. Valliere
Christine LaSala
Alan G. Page
Willis T. King, Jr.
William C. Bauman
John W. Gussenhoven
William C. Remington
Edward J. Buchwald
James W. McElvany
Rufus J. Williams III
S. Robert Beane
William S. Jennings
Gerald R. Swanson
John V. Deitchman
Theodore J. Fuller

Elected January 1, 1995:

John A. McMahon

Christian Dahms
   Jauch & Hübener

Santiago Gil de Biedma
   Gil y Carvajal

Patrick Lucas
   Gras Savoye

MANAGING PRINCIPALS AS OF YEAR-END 1994

Seated, from left to right:

Herbert R. Selander, Jr.
Craig A. Clements
Lawrence I. Geneen
John A. McMahon
Thomas N. Pappas

Standing, from left to right:

Richard B. Blackman
George J. Kadri
D. Darby Duryea
John E. Jenniges
Dan Knise
Fred L. Packer
James B. Meathe
Daniel L. Jones
Robert F. O'Leary
J. Cameron Campbell
Fernand Baruch, Jr.
Brooke N. Williams
William J. Keckeisen

Not Shown:

Aad S. Strijbos

Elected January 1, 1995:

Donald H. Birdsong
William M. Choate
Paul P. Giunto
Kenneth J. Goodchild

RETIRED DIRECTORS

1. Sam W. Aiena
2. Lloyd H. Benedict
3. Peter A. Bergsten
4. William J. Bumsted
5. Prescott S. Bush, Jr.
6. Robert A. Cameron
7. Hawley T. Chester, Jr.
8. Gilbert H. Dunham
9. Robert L. Hannon, Jr.
10. Robert V. Hatcher, Jr.
11. Kenneth A. Hecken
12. Harvey M. Kelsey, Jr.
13. George F.B. Owens, Jr.
14. Richard J. Rice
15. J. Kenneth Seward
16. Gustave S. Werner
17. Walter H. Clemens
18. John H. McEown
19. Dickinson C. Ross
20. E. Eric Johnson
21. George D. Benjamin
22. Kenneth K. Keene
23. Edwin L. Knetzger, Jr.
24. Richard E. Meyer
25. Richard I. Purnell
26. George F. Shattuck, Jr.

(see chart below)

Not Shown:

Thomas L. Avegno
Peter B. Bickett
John H. Dowling
William T. Dunn, Jr.
Edward F. Feuge
Baxter Gentry
Edmond S. Gillette, Jr.
Denver C. Ginsey
James G. Harlow
W. Mitchell LaMotte
Richard A. Mittnacht
Charles Page
John N. Robinson
David H. Winton

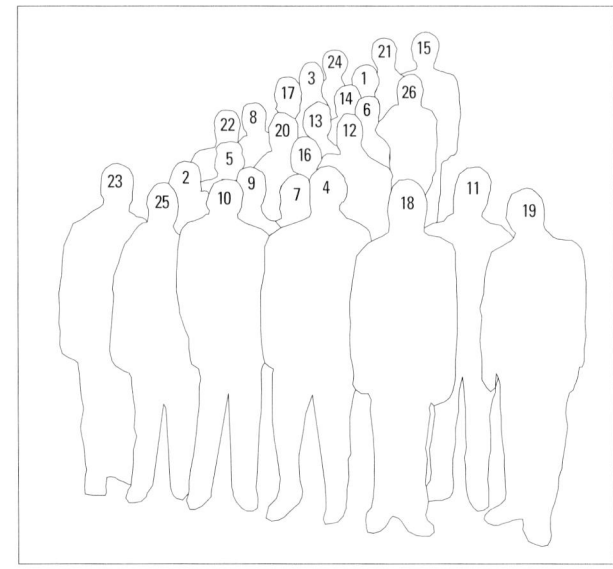

DIRECTORS: 1845-1995

Became a partner or Director		Retired (R) Died in Office (D)		Became a partner or Director		Retired (R) Died in Office (D)		Became a partner or Director		Retired (R) Died in Office (D)	
1845	Walter R. Jones, Jr.	R	1854	1946	Louis Tofte	R	1956	1978	George F. B. Owens, Jr.	R	1990
1845	Henry W. Johnson	D	1881	1947	Howard F. Quigley	R	1963	1979	Peter B. Bickett	R	1985
1854	A. Foster Higgins	R	1887	1947	Clifford C. Thomas	D	1958	1979	Peter M. Black	Res.	1983
1874	A. William Krebs	R	1901	1948	Cletus Keating	R	1961	1979	Harvey M. Kelsey, Jr.	R	1985
1882	John Barrett	D	1920	1949	Earle E. Baruch	D	1962	1979	Richard E. Meyer	R	1993
1885	John H. Gourlie, Jr.	R	1900	1949	Dorrance Sexton	R	1972	1980	David A. Olsen	—	—
1887	James B. Dickson	R	1919	1950	Mortimer M. Denker	R	1965	1980	E. Massie Valentine	—	—
1892	Stephen Loines	R	1918	1951	Paul M. Corbett	R	1970	1981	David W. Bianchi	—	—
1894	William Curtin	R	1926	1951	John S. Wiester	R	1968	1981	Gilbert H. Dunham	R	1991
1894	William E. Lowe	R	1910	1953	C. Stewart Anderson	R	1971	1981	John P. Keyser	—	—
1898	William Brockie	D	1909	1954	Alexander Olsen	R	1962	1981	Albert S. McGhee	R	1994
1900	Robert P. Lethbridge	D	1908	1956	J. Baxter Gentry	R	1971	1981	Rodney D. Day III	—	—
1900	William H. Davidge	R	1923	1956	C. Ward Chase	R	1969	1981	Gardner M. Mundy	—	—
1901	Frank G. Macomber	R	1905	1956	Roby Harrington, Jr.	R	1970	1982	Richard A. Nielsen	—	—
1901	Stephen C. Hunter	R	1919	1957	John N. Robinson	R	1975	1982	Thomas G. Patzau	—	—
1903	William R. Coe	R	1943	1958	David H. Winton	R	1979	1982	J. Kenneth Seward	R	1993
1905	W.H. LaBoyteaux	D	1947	1960	Sherwood M. Bonney	R	1972	1982	George H. Shattuck, Jr.	R	1992
1907	George V. Coe	R	1943	1962	William J. Bumsted	R	1979	1983	Richard J. Rice	R	1990
1908	John A.H. Hopkins	R	1920	1963	Richard T. Henshaw, Jr.	R	1977	1983	Kennard B. Ross	R	1984
1910	William H. Botsford	R	1923	1963	Richard I. Purnell	R	1981	1983	Sam W. Aiena	R	1993
1910	William N. Davey	R	1947	1964	Henry E. Cabaud, Jr.	R	1974	1984	James D. Altman	—	—
1910	Henry W. Lowe	R	1948	1964	Edward F. Feuge	R	1975	1985	James W. McElvany	—	—
1911	Thomas J. Prindiville	R	1918	1965	Clark T. Foster	D	1971	1985	Gerald R. Swanson	—	—
1916	John S. Keegan	R	1949	1965	Edwin L. Knetzger, Jr.	R	1985	1986	Burt N. Sempier	Res.	1991
1920	Herbert B. Sexton	R	1948	1965	Richard A. Mittnacht	R	1982	1987	S. Robert Beane	—	—
1921	William E. Hall	R	1950	1965	Dickinson C. Ross	R	1985	1987	William S. Jennings	—	—
1924	Louis F. Becker	R	1932	1966	John L. Baringer	R	1976	1987	Martin L. Rayner	D	1994
1924	John A. Bishop	R	1930	1966	Hawley T. Chester, Jr.	R	1981	1987	Norman Barham	—	—
1924	Alexander Field	R	1943	1966	William T. Dunn, Jr.	R	1982	1987	Willis T. King, Jr.	—	—
1924	E.A. Hasson	R	1927	1966	Edmond S. Gillette, Jr.	R	1981	1988	Edward J. Buchwald	R	1995
1924	Ernest W. Congdon	D	1928	1966	Robert L. Hannon, Jr.	R	1981	1988	Theodore J. Fuller	—	—
1924	Elmer F. Hunt	R	1932	1968	E. Eric Johnson	R	1987	1988	Joseph D. Roxe	—	—
1924	Ernest P. Lenihan	R	1928	1969	Prescott S. Bush, Jr.	R	1984	1989	John W. Gussenhoven	—	—
1924	Raymond T. Marshall	R	1945	1969	John H. Dowling	R	1977	1989	Brian R. Hall	—	—
1924	Robert J. Taylor	D	1943	1970	John H. McEown	R	1985	1989	Robert F. Powell, Jr.	—	—
1924	H. Nottingham Townsend	D	1927	1971	Gustave S. Werner	R	1985	1989	William C. Remington	R	1995
1927	Lewis A. Wallace	R	1940	1972	Lloyd Benedict	R	1984	1990	Alan G. Page	—	—
1931	W.E.J. Ord	R	1951	1972	Beverly M. DuBose, Jr.	R	1981	1990	Joseph P. Platt, Jr.	—	—
1933	Reginald W. Cauchois	R	1953	1972	Denver C. Ginsey	R	1986	1990	Rufus J. Williams III	—	—
1933	Andrew Friberg	R	1943	1972	Kenneth K. Keene	R	1987	1991	William C. Bauman	—	—
1939	H.H. Salmon, Jr.	R	1956	1972	Thomas L. Avegno	R	1978	1991	Richard E. Valliere	—	—
1940	Courtlandt Otis	R	1964	1973	Thomas E. Barton	D	1980	1993	John V. Deitchman	—	—
1941	R.B.H. Chapman	Res.	1946	1974	Peter A. Bergsten	R	1992	1993	Christine LaSala	—	—
1942	Monroe Maltby	R	1965	1975	James G. Harlow	R	1988	1995	John A. McMahon	—	—
1943	Elmer L. Jefferson	R	1962	1975	Robert V. Hatcher, Jr.	R	1990	1995	Christian Dahms Jauch & Hübener	—	—
1943	Charles R. Nash	R	1955	1975	Kenneth A. Hecken	R	1991				
1943	E.P. Crossan	R	1963	1976	Walter H. Clemens	R	1990	1995	Santiago Gil de Biedma Gil y Carvajal	—	—
1944	Frank S. Symons	R	1955	1977	Robert A. Cameron	R	1990				
1944	Charles Page	R	1964	1977	George D. Benjamin	R	1993	1995	Patrick Lucas Gras Savoye	—	—
1945	Henry I. Bernard	Res.	1955	1977	W. Mitchell LaMotte	R	1992				
				1977	Palmer D. Sparkman	D	1979				

Index

A

Aetna Insurance Company, 73
Aiena, Sam W., **138**
Altman, James D., 72, 118, **136**
Aluminum Company of America, 87
American Foreign Insurance Association, 78
American President Lines, 51
Anderson, C. Stewart "Pop", 60
Andrea Doria, **110**
Appleton, James D., 123
Association of Average Adjusters of the United States, 25, 43
Atlantic Life Insurance Company, 100
Atlantic Mutual Insurance Company, 20, 24, 31, 32
Avegno, Thomas L., 138
Average adjusting, 23, 25

B

Balderston, Elizabeth J., 122, 125
Barham, Norman, 116, 135, **136**
Barrett, John D., 36, 111
Baruch, Earle, 42, 87
Baruch, Fernand, Jr., **137**
Bauman, William C., 118, **136**
Beane, S. Robert, 81, 84, **136**
Benedict, Lloyd, 68, 75, 78, 80, **138**
Benjamin, George D., **138**
Bergsten, Peter A., **138**
Berkowitz, Sandra L., 135
Bertolacci, Charles E., 134
Bianchi, David W., **136**
Bickett, Peter B., 78, 138
Binford, Charles M., 12, 17, 72
Birdsong, Donald H., 137
Blackman, Richard B., **137**
Boeing Company, 13, **15**,
Bradford, William L., 123
British and Foreign Marine Insurance Company, 50
Brockie, William, 42
Brockman y Schuh, 95
Buchwald, Edward J., **136**
Bumsted, William J., 80, **138**
Bush, Prescott S., Jr., **138**

C

Cabaud, Henry, 129
Cameron, Robert A., **138**
Campbell, J. Cameron, **137**
Carlson, Don, 13, 72, 78, 108
Carter Brito e Cunha, 98, 109, 113, 115
Cartright, Alexander, 22
Cassedy, John H., 110
Cauchois, Reginald W., 68, 70
Chan, Alice Tak-Hing, 84
Charles, Joan, 101
Chase, C. Ward, 60, 63
Chester, Hawley T., Jr., 60, **138**
Chicago fire, **39**, 41
Choate, William M., 137
Chrysler Corporation, 71, 78
Clemens, Walter H., 132, **138**
Clements, Craig A., **137**
Cleveland, Grover, 36
Cody, William F. "Buffalo Bill", 44
Coe, George, 42, 43, 44, 55
Coe, Mai Rogers, 43-44
Coe, William R., 33, **42**, 43-44, 51, 55
Colgate-Palmolive Company, 78, 80
College of Insurance, 100
Cunard Steamship Company, 52
Cunningham, Charles, 41-42, 87
Curland, Charles W., 63
Curtin, William W., 41, 42
Curtin & Brockie, 28, 42

D

Dahms, Christian, 80, **82**, 102, 115, 127, 136
Davey, William N., 55, 58
Davis, Roberta A., 134
Day, Rodney D. III, 13, 41, 88, 95, 122, 125, 130, **136**
Deitchman, John V., 119, **136**
DiBona, Christine, 119
Denker, Morton M., 60, 132
Dickson, James B., 41, 108
Doremus & Company, 46
Dowling, John H., 138
Dunham, Gilbert H., **138**
Dunn, William T., Jr., 138
Duryea, D. Darby, 135, **137**

E

Eastman Kodak Company, 37, 122
Edison, Thomas, 25
Elliott, Roger, 113, 114
Erie Canal, 20
Exxon Corporation, 37

F

Faison, Seth, 41, 56, 71, 103
Farrell Lines, 51
Feuge, Edward F., 138
Fireman's Fund Insurance Company, 55
Fluor Corporation, 119
Flying Cloud, 27, **29**
Foster Higgins (A. Foster Higgins & Co.), 131, 132-133
Fuller, Theodore J., **136**

G

Geisbush, Tip, 135
Geneen, Lawrence I., **137**
General Motors Corporation, 63
Gentry, Baxter, 73, 138
Gillett, Roger, 95
Gillette, Edmond S., Jr., 138
Gillette Company, 71
Gil de Biedma, Santiago, 80, 103, **136**
Gil y Carvajal, 80, 103, 136
Ginsey, Denver C., 65, 70, 138
Giunto, Paul P., **137**
Global Capital Reinsurance Limited, 131
Goldberg, L. John, 93, 112
Goldman, Sachs & Co., 16, 105
Goodchild, Kenneth J., 137
Goodyear Tire & Rubber Company, 63
Gormley, Matthew, 60, 63, 65
Gourlie, John H., Jr., 41
Gras Savoye, 81, 84, 136
Great American Insurance Company, 129
GTE Corporation, 91, 123
Gussenhoven, John W., 127, **136**

H

Hall, Brian R., 90, 91, 93, 95, **136**
Hall, William E., 63
Hannon, Robert L., Jr., **138**
Harlow, James G., 138
Harrington, Roby, Jr., 60, 63, 78
Hatcher, Martha Anne, 105
Hatcher, Robert V., Jr., 31, 70, 84, **89**, 96-105, **97**, **99**, **100**, 113, 114, 127, 130, **138**
Hecken, Kenneth A., 84, 98, 114, **138**
Henshaw, Richard T., Jr., 60, 71-72, 75, 101, 129
Henry W. Johnson, **31**, 33
Henry Ward Johnson & Co., 120
Higgins, Andrew Foster, **11**, **20**, 25, **30**, 31, 36
Higgins, Sara, **20**, **30**
Hollmeyer, Harry, 75, 77
Home Insurance Company, 83
Howard, Frederic, 36
Hudson, Mike J., 17
Hunt, Elmer F., 57, 60, 67
Hyman, Allen F., 135

I

India House, 51
Insurance Company of North America, 73
Insurance Services Division (ISD), 119
International Insurance Inc., 81

J

Jauch & Hübener, 80, 81, 84, 102, 115, 127, 136
Jefferson, Elmer L., 66-68, **67**, 71, 72, 74, **89**
Jenniges, John E., **137**
Jennings, William S., **136**
J&H University, 123, 131
Johnson, E. Eric, 60, 132, **138**
Johnson, Henry Ward, **10**, 25, 31, 36, 43
Johnson & Higgins: Adjusting Department, 42, 55, 61, 65; Atlanta office, 68, 88; Baltimore office, 43, 45; Beijing office, 84; Boston office, 31, 45; captives management, 90-95; Casualty Department, 43, 46, 57, 63, 72, 78; Charlotte office, 88; Chicago office, 63, 65, 70, 73, 78, 83, 88, 125, 129, 134, 135; Cleveland office, 67, 125; corporate structure, 16-17, 36-37; Costa Mesa office, 119; Denver office, 71; Detroit office, 70, 71, 78; Employee Benefits Department, 60, 65, 105, 132; Fire Department, 43; Grand Rapids office, 78; Great Depression, impact on J&H, 46; Hartford office, 71; Havana office, 74; Houston office, 71, 129-130, 135; International Department, 78, 81, 83; international expansion, 68, 74-89, 102-103; Junior Advisory Committee, 53; Lima office, 83; London office, 115, 135; Los Angeles office, 12, 60, 63, 77, 134, 135; Marine Department, 42, 53, 60, 63, 68, 72, 80, 87; Minneapolis office, 68; Nashville office, 88; New Orleans office, 45, 63, 65, 71; New York office, 41, 51; one-hundredth anniversary, 47, **48-49**; Philadelphia office, 28, 41-42, 50, 63, 78, 87, 88, 105, 135; Phoenix office, 72, 88; Pittsburgh office, 68, 87, 120, 135; Portland (Oregon) office, 71; private ownership, 17, 67-68, 103, 105; Property Department, 17, 57, 60, 65, 78; Quality initiative, 16, 121, 122-125, 131; reinsurance brokerage, 98; relationships with underwriters, 13, 61, 72, 87; retained earnings, 16; Richmond office, 71, 96, 101-102; Rio de Janeiro office, 75-77; San Francisco office, 40, 41, 51, 65, 78, 88, 129; St. Louis office, 13, 108; Seattle office, 65, 88, 118, 134; "single treasury" philosophy, 88; Stamford office, 125, 135; technology, use of, 119-121; Tokyo office, 81; Tulsa office, 88; United States retail operations, 116-121; Washington, D.C., office, 119, 123; Wilmington office, 68
Johnson & Higgins (Canada) Ltd., 83
Johnson & Higgins Financial Services, 132
Johnson & Higgins Global Captive Management Group, 90-95, 92
Johnson & Higgins Intermediaries, 93
Johnson & Higgins (Quebec) Limited, 80
Johnson & Higgins, S.p.A. (Italy), 80-81
Johnson & Johnson, 71
Jones, Daniel L., **137**
Jones & Johnson, 23
Jones, Walter Restored, 20
Jones, Walter Restored, Jr., **20**, 31

K

Kadri, George J., **137**
Keckeisen, William J., **137**
Keegan, John S., 61
Keene, Kenneth K., **138**
Kelley, Dixon W., 51, 55, 57, 61, 63
Kelley, Lyn S., 125
Kelley, Margaret, 55
Kelsey, Harvey M., Jr., 60, **138**
Keyser, John P., 65, 134, **136**
King, Willis T., Jr., 98, **136**
Klepp, Walter E., 63, 73
Knetzger, Edwin L., Jr., 60, 105, 132, **138**
Knise, Dan, 123, **137**
Kratovil, Emil A., 70
Krebs, A. William, 36

L

LaBoyteaux, William H., 42, 44, 45, 46-47, **50**, 50-55, 57, 60, 68, 98, 112
LaMotte, W. Mitchell, 60, 138
LaSala, Christine, 16, 123, 127, **136**
Linde, Michael, 135
Lloyd, Jim, 78
Lloyd's of London, 73, 80, **108**, **109**, 111
Logue, Karen R., 135
Loines, Stephen, 111
Lucas, Patrick, 81, **82**, 136

M

McElvany, James W., 12, **136**
McEown, John H., 129, 130, 132, **138**
McGhee, Albert S., **136**
McGowan, Thomas J., 110
McMahon, John A., 136, **137**
McNally, Michael J., 87
Meathe, James B., **137**
Mees & zoonen, 80
Mellon, Andrew, 13, **14**
Mercury astronauts, 13, **14**
Meyer, Richard E., 90, 91, 93, 95, 108, 114-115, **138**
Meyers, Robert K., 135
Mittnacht, Richard A., 60, 67, 68, 70, 129, 138
Morgan, J.P., Sr., 36, 37
Morgan Stanley, 105
Morro Castle, 34
Morse, Samuel, 22
Mundy, Gardner, 16, 36, 57, 89, 95, 102, **136**

N

National Association of Insurance Brokers, 114
Nelson, John P., 53, 61
Nielsen, Richard A., 47, 60, 88, 93, 99, 115, **117**, 118, 119, 121, 122, 123, 125, 130, **136**

O

O'Leary, Robert F., **137**
Olsen, Alexander, 53, 61, 127
Olsen, Bobbie, 127
Olsen, David A., 13, 16, 17, 25, 60, 70, 72, **82**, 95, 105, 113, 114, 115, 116, 118, 125, 126-131, **128**, **136**
Olympic Games, 13
Ord, Eric, 51
Otis, Courtlandt, 57, 63
Owens, George F. B., Jr., 63, **138**

P

Packer, Fred L., **137**
Page, Alan G., 119, **136**
Page, Charles, 50, 51, 55, 67, 70, 138
Palmer, David, 113
Pappas, Thomas N., **137**
Patzau, Thomas G., **136**
Peck, David F., 125
Pennzoil Company, 91
Petrie, Robert G. III, 95, 121
Pierson, Jennifer, 119
Planting Fields, 44
Platt, Joseph P., Jr., 116, **136**
Poe, Edgar Allen, 22, **22**
Polk, James, **22**
Portaria, Rudi, 83
Powell, Robert F., Jr., 132-133, **136**
Purnell, Maggie, 89
Purnell, Richard I., 42, 60, 63, 66, 68, 72, 74, 75, 81, 86-89, **86**, **89**, 90, 96, **97**, 99, 102, 113, 127, 129, 130, **138**

Q

Quaker Oats Company, 37
Queen of the Pacific, **40**, 41
Quigley, Howard F., 53, 60

R

Rainbow, **22**
Rainoff, George, 81
Reiss, Fred, 91
Remington, William C., **136**
Rice, Richard J., 57, 91, 99, **138**
Robinson, John N., 138
Ross, Dickinson C., 60, 63, 65, 87, **138**
Roxe, Joseph D., 16, 17, 60, **136**

S

Salmon, June, Jr., 46, 53
San Francisco earthquake, **39**
Sauer, Susan M., 125, 135
Schneider, Bob, 135
Secretariat, 13, **15**,
Selander, Herbert R., Jr., **137**
Seward, J. Kenneth, 77, 80, 81-84, **138**
Sexton, Dorrance, 42, 53, 56, 60, 66, 68-71, **69**, 72, 74, 75, 78, 80, 81, 84, 86, 87, 88, **89**, 99, 101
Sexton, Herbert B., 68
Shattuck, George F., Jr., **138**
Shipowners Claims Bureau, 25, 110
Sibson & Company, 131
Sirotzky, Sara, 83
Southall, Len, 112
Sparkman, Palmer, 129
Spencer, Edwin J., 111
Squibb Corporation, 71
Standard Oil, 43, 77
Stephenson, Patrick J. T., 80
Strijbos, Aad S., 137
Stryker Corporation, 78
Sullivan & Cromwell, 104, 131
Swanson, Gerald R., 118, **136**

T

Texas Instruments Incorporated, 71
3M Corporation, 77-78
Time, Incorporated, 13
Titanic, 13, **14**, 33, **34**, **35**
Tokio Marine & Fire, 81
Toyota, 135
Transatlantic Marine Insurance Company of Berlin, 28
Tregoe, Benjamin B., 102
Tyson, John D., 111, 112

U

UNISON, 13, 16, 81-84, 90, 95, 100, 103, 108, 114, 127, 131, 135
United States Lines, 51
United States Steel, 36

V

Vaccarino, James M., 31
Valentine, E. Massie, 100, 101, **136**
Valliere, Richard E., **136**
Varuna, 32, **33**

W

Warner-Lambert Company, 71
Wells, Gideon, 32, 33
Werner, Gustave S., **138**
Whitmore, Howard B., 135
Wiester, John S., 60, 63, 65
Willcox Incorporated Reinsurance Intermediaries, 98
Willcox, Peck & Hughes, 42, 112
Williams, Brooke N., **137**
Williams, Rufus J. III, 89, 120, **136**
Willis, Faber & Co., 34, 63, 84, 98, 106-115
Wilson, William W. III, 120
Winter, William D., 32
Winton, David H., 13, 46-47, 63, 67, 72, 112, 138
Wood, Alexander "Sandy", 55, 61, 63
Wreaks, Charles A., 111

Y

Yankee clippers, 22, 27
Yates, Alfred, 39

Z

Zimmerman, John W., 102

Boldface listings indicate photographs.

Acknowledgments

In researching and writing this book, the author interviewed nearly 150 current and retired employees and clients of the firm, and without exception they were generous in their help and enthusiastic in their support. The author wishes to thank each of them. Special thanks are owed to Jane Krumrine and Gunther Marx, who helped guide the author from start to finish.

In addition, the author gratefully acknowledges the following sources:

The First Hundred Years of an American Institution: The Story of Johnson & Higgins, Insurance Brokers and Average Adjusters, from 1845 to 1945, published privately by Johnson & Higgins, 1945; reprinted, 1983.

Cosgrove, John N., *Gray Days and Gold: A Character Sketch of Atlantic Mutual Insurance Company*, published privately by the Atlantic Mutual Companies, 1967.

Powell, Edward W., *Red Skies... Morning and Night: A History of the Atlantic Mutual Companies*, published privately by the Atlantic Mutual Companies, 1992.

Winton, David Holt, *Recollections of Johnson & Higgins: 1935-1979*, Canaan, New Hampshire: Phoenix Publishing, 1987.

Videotaped interviews conducted by Rodney D. Day III with Charles P. Cunningham and Richard I. Purnell.

Videotaped interviews conducted by Seth Faison with Peter B. Bickett, Walter H. Clemens, Edwin L. Knetzger, Jr., Richard I. Purnell and Dorrance Sexton.